MULTIDIMENSIONAL
EXECUTIVE COACHING

RUTH L. ORENSTEIN, PsyD, consults, teaches, researches, and writes in the area of organizational psychology, specializing in executive development at the individual and group level. She is president of Princeton Consulting Resources, Inc. (PCRI), a member of the part-time faculties of Rutgers University's Graduate School of Applied and Professional Psychology and the Wharton School's Aresty Institute of Executive Education, and a founding board member of the Graduate School Alliance for Executive Coaching.

Dr. Orenstein has extensive consulting experience in both corporate and nonprofit organizations and has provided executive coaching to hundreds of senior leaders. She has held senior line-management positions in several Fortune corporations and, prior to founding PCRI, was a senior vice president at the Chemical Banking Corporation, with full profit-and-loss responsibility for the retail branch system in central and southern New Jersey. She has taught courses in management and organizational psychology at the graduate and undergraduate levels at the New School for Social Research, Adelphi University, and Rutgers University, where she also created and directed the Organizational Psychology Consulting Group at the Center for Applied Psychology.

Dr. Orenstein is a Phi Beta Kappa graduate of Queens College (City University of New York) with a BA in English literature and holds an MS in management from the University of Utah and a PsyD in organizational psychology from Rutgers University. She has published several landmark articles on executive coaching and is the recipient of the American Psychological Association's RHR International Outstanding Dissertation Award for her work, *Executive Coaching: An Integrative Model.*

Multidimensional Executive Coaching

Ruth L. Orenstein, PsyD

SPRINGER PUBLISHING COMPANY

NEW YORK

Springer Publishing Company, LLC
11 West 42nd Street
New York, NY 10036
www.springerpub.com

Acquisitions Editor: Sheri W. Sussman
Project Manager: Carol Cain
Cover design: Mimi Flow
Composition: Apex Publishing, LLC

07 08 09 10/ 5 4 3 2 1

Library of Congress Cataloging-in-Publication Data

Orenstein, Ruth L.
   Multidimensional executive coaching / Ruth L. Orenstein.
      p. cm.
   Includes bibliographical references.
   ISBN-13: 978-0-8261-2566-8 (alk. paper)
   ISBN-10: 0-8261-2566-2 (alk. paper)
   1. Executive coaching.   2. Organizational change.   3. Organizational
effectiveness.   I. Title.

HD30.4.O743 2007
658.4'07124—dc22   2007005890

Printed in the United States of America by Bang Printing

This book is dedicated to Nathan Friedman and Stanley Orenstein
in loving and grateful memory

Contents

Part I. Multidimensional Executive Coaching: Foundations

Part II. Multidimensional Executive Coaching: The Practice

Phase I. Entry

List of Figures and Tables

Figures

Tables

Foreword

This is a wise book in several ways.

First of all, it describes the work of a wise practitioner who is able to provide exceptionally thoughtful and reliable help to her clients, synthesizing a complex and diverse array of perspectives in the process.

Ruth Orenstein sees individuals shrewdly and deeply, targeting their capacity to receive the help she can offer and, in response, adapt and change their behaviors at work. But she also understands the organizations in which they work, the factors that constrain their effectiveness and also provide the opportunities for them to succeed. Sizing up the work environments in which problems arise, she is able to discriminate where the real difficulties lie, helping her clients to see the ways in which she can best help them. Many clients tend to blame themselves for their difficulties—that is, if they don't entirely blame others. Orenstein demonstrates again and again that she can see through the confusion and pain she is presented with—as well as the misleading certainties—and discern the underlying issues.

She also understands herself and how her reactions provide important clues as to the meaning of what her clients say and do. This may be her most important talent, the source of her most reliable insights into what is really going on. Knowing herself, she can see more clearly into the hearts and minds of others. Trusting her own reactions and perceptions, she can know what to trust in others, what to believe, and what to question.

But this is not merely the effect of a unique and ineffable talent. It is the product of training and hard work in mastering several crucially important disciplines. This is the second way in which this book is wise: it introduces us to the concepts, the research, the practices, and traditions that have informed Orenstein's own professional development. She allows us to see that there is no mystery or accident behind her success. She makes clear that these ways of thinking and working, developed over many years by a number of serious professionals, have enabled her to become a skilled and thoughtful practitioner—and they can also enable others as well. Education and training are the keys to effective coaching in the "multidimensional" approach this book describes, and she lets us know clearly what is involved.

This does not diminish Orenstein's achievement in any way. She is an immensely talented, empathic, and creative person who has brought those qualities to her training and her work. Not everyone has what she has, certainly in the requisite degree. The work of coaching she describes is not for the indifferently equipped or marginally talented. But for those who have the talent, she has shown the way.

She has also described with exceptional clarity how these multiple dimensions of individual psychoanalytic, group dynamics, and systems thinking impinge on each other and interpenetrate in practice. Even those who are familiar with the thinking she describes can learn from how she moves deftly among these perspectives, shifting her focus as her work with individual clients dictates. Her ideas have been honed by years of effective practice.

Even so, with this arsenal of tools and the various strategies they suggest, one cannot always succeed. Not everyone actually wants to be helped or is open to the ideas and insights required to change their behavior. Moreover, not every organization that brings in a coach, ostensibly to "help" a distressed or promising executive, actually wants that person to succeed. They may believe they do, and they may be willing to pay for help, but that hardly means a willingness to face the problems that have been located in those persons or reassess the dilemmas assigned to those sectors of the organization. And that is part of wisdom, too: to try one's best to help but be willing to walk away from jobs that cannot be done or to refuse assignments of dubious value. Orenstein has been through these difficult straits again and again, and she has much of value to say about them.

This book is particularly valuable today. Coaching addresses an important and growing need as businesses and other organizations face unprecedented pressures, not only from the market but also from new technologies and rapid demographic shifts. As a field of practice, it has expanded at an extraordinary rate, offering help for beleaguered executives at a time when corporate hierarchies are constantly shifting and the informal networks of mentors and colleagues that once provided guidance and support have been substantially eroded. Executives crave help—so long as it is not seen as a sign of incompetence or failure—and corporations are eager to provide it, as busy senior executives often want to avoid becoming enmeshed in relations with those who report to them. I also think they frequently want to avoid what they do not have the time or patience to provide themselves, and often look forward to engaging experts who they can believe have the understanding and skills they lack. To put it bluntly, much of coaching today is mentoring outsourced.

On the other side, coaching attracts many who have convinced themselves that they understand the skills needed for success, or who have gone through brief training that promises such understanding. It is frequently asserted that it has nothing to do with psychotherapy, the neighboring form of help that inevitably comes to mind as an analogy if not a model. As Orenstein makes clear, it is entirely true that coaching is distinct from therapy, and the coach has to keep the distinction in mind. At the same time, effective coaching runs up against similar problems and requires comparable skills at reading behavior and negotiating relationships that depend on openness and trust. Quick and superficial training, glib self-confidence, even a reasonably good track-record as a manager is not enough in knowing how to help another person and dealing with the pitfalls of understanding complex motivations.

Today, many are all too eager to earn the lucrative fees that are frequently paid for this work. As a result, the field is immensely diverse, unorganized, unregulated, and filled with well-intentioned practitioners with questionable and, frequently, superficial skills. As a psychoanalyst who frequently works in the business environment, I know that people bring their problems with them to work. Even top executives with successful records can have difficulty exercising calm and decisive judgment. Moreover, like the rest of us, they can often also have difficulty seeing clearly what they are up against. In this respect the world of work is just another part of the world we live in. And change is difficult. Fear is inevitably evoked and resistances are usually engaged. Yes, it might be easy to teach someone to organize his or her desk or convey useful tips in running a meeting—but often the problems are much deeper than that. How many coaches really understand that or are seriously prepared to look more deeply into their client's reactions? Pep talks are seldom enough.

Organizations, moreover, have little ability to know what they are getting for their money. And here is where Orenstein demonstrates her wisdom in yet another way, providing means of assessment. Not only does she appreciate the complexity of the issues to be encountered at work, she understands the ease with which practitioners and clients can be deceived into believing that they have accomplished more than they actually have. A client may never know the help he did not get. He or she may wonder about it or feel disappointed, but coaches who are all too eager to believe in their effectiveness can easily reassure them that they are doing "just great!" A lively and engaging personality can cover a multitude of sins, with clients ending up feeling that, once again, they simply lack the basic stuff needed to understand and overcome their problems.

Orenstein has built into her approach evaluative measures that guard against such collusions. Clients and the organizations that pay for services can get a read on how it worked and when it did not. The wise practitioner not only wants clients to understand and evaluate what they are getting, she wants to know herself, and she will search for means to find out.

Wisdom in this realm is all too hard to come by. But here it is, both for those who want to know where to find it, so they can use it, and for those who want to know how to acquire it.

Kenneth Eisold, PhD
Past President, International Society for
the Psychoanalytic Study of Organizations

Preface

Shortly before beginning work on this book, the following three incidents occurred:

- I received a call from the human relations director of a well-known foundation. "I heard you speak at a recent convention," she said, "and I need your advice. We are planning to provide executive coaching to our senior managers. There are so many people who call themselves 'executive coaches' that I am not sure what qualifications I should be looking for."
- During a meeting concerning strategy for executive development at a Fortune 50 corporation, the company's director of leadership development commented, "We have spent hundreds of thousands of dollars on coaching over the course of the last five years. We have coaches who have been with us that long. And we still do not have a way to evaluate the cost effectiveness of the money we are spending."
- Asked to teach a doctoral-level course on executive coaching at a major university, I searched the literature for relevant intellectual material. I was forced to conclude that nothing appropriate existed in the current public domain.

The need for documenting a disciplined, theory-based approach for the effective practice of executive coaching has been made evident to me by these and a myriad of other incidents. This book is my attempt to address that need by presenting the conceptual framework for the practice of and the practical considerations regarding an approach I have named (hopefully aptly) "multi-dimensional executive coaching."

The book is composed of five parts. Part I is the foundational material. The first chapter, which serves as a reference point for ensuing chapters, is an in-depth case history. The second chapter defines executive coaching and examines the current state of the field. It includes a literature review as well as reasons for the explosive growth in the practice. The third chapter explicates the guiding theory, with particular emphasis on the following: the psychological determinants of individual behavior; role theory; the impact of conscious and unconscious organizational forces on individual behavior; the group-as-a-whole phenomenon and its influence on the individual; embedded intergroup relations and the unconscious effects of identity and organizational group memberships; and the concept of the consultant's use of self as tool, including how rigorous self-reflection by the executive coach informs the entire executive coaching process.

Part II describes the actual practice of executive coaching based on the guiding theory presented in Part I. It explains the process in its entirety, from initial contact through termination, and makes extensive use of examples from, and analyses of, actual case histories. Phase I, "Entry," discusses the initial contact with the organization, the first meeting with the client, the formulation of the preliminary coaching plan, and the executive coaching contract, as well as the crucial data that can be gleaned about the organization and the client from these first contacts. Phase II, "Facilitating Change," is the heart of the coaching process. "Assessment" presents four methods for assessing behavior: the unstructured interview with the client; semistructured, qualitative 360-degree interviews; unstructured observation; and the coach's use of self. Analysis of the data, including attention to reliability and validity, is also thoroughly discussed. "Feedback," the next chapter, encompasses the process of giving feedback to the client (both orally and in written form) in a way that the client can best absorb it. It also explains how feedback is given from the perspective of multi-level forces impacting the perceptions of the client's behavior. "Objectives Setting" discusses the formulation of specific coaching objectives based on the feedback, both individually with the client and then in a joint meeting with the manager to whom the client reports—and the rich data that can be illuminated from such a meeting. "Formal Coaching" describes the one-on-one work with the client to achieve the stated objectives. The chapter includes a guide for conducting coaching meetings, a compendium of coaching techniques, and a range of examples that demonstrate the depth and breadth of coaching interventions that must be in the coach's repertoire and the factors that must be considered when using each one.

In Phase III, "Concluding Coaching," the topic of outcome evaluation (which, at the time of this writing, is still conspicuous by its absence in executive coaching literature) is discussed. The chapter includes specific, practical, and statistically sound methods for evaluating the effectiveness of coaching. Techniques for concluding the coaching process are examined in the following chapter.

Part III of the book, "Practical Considerations," considers two broad areas—potential coaching failures (i.e., when to decline or exit a coaching assignment) and implications for practice, including the education and training of executive coaches and ethical dilemmas in the field.

Part IV, the final section, summarizes and then uses the concepts and techniques discussed throughout the book in a detailed analysis of the case history presented in the first chapter. As further aids for the reader, there are appendices with sample documents relevant for practice and annotated bibliographies at the conclusion of each chapter for further reading and investigation.

Twelve years ago, I took the ultimate professional leap of faith when, midcareer, I abandoned the executive suite to return to the classroom full time. My purpose was to equip myself with the knowledge and skill to alleviate the debilitating psychological pain I both witnessed and experienced throughout the workplace. It is my fervent hope that this book will be used as a vehicle to expand the knowledge and skill base for those who wish to do the same. It is offered to the reader in that spirit.

Acknowledgments

First and foremost, I would like to thank the two people most impacted by my decision to write this book. I thank Tony Gabriel, the love of my life, for reminding me of the reasons for continuing to write at those times when I was all too ready to forget them, and for his caring and patient support throughout the effort. And I thank Vicki Lincoln, my business partner and "soul sister," for always being there to share in the frustrations and the successes and always knowing the right thing to say and do, professionally and personally.

This book would not have been possible without the education and training I received in the organizational psychology program at the Graduate School of Applied and Professional Psychology at Rutgers University. I am indebted to Clayton P. Alderfer, Kenwyn Smith (at the University of Pennsylvania), Karen Riggs Skean, and Nancy Fagley for introducing me to ways of thinking that deeply influence the way in which I work; to Cary Cherniss and Lew Gantwerk for continually encouraging expansion of the work; and to my friends and colleagues throughout my studies, particularly Andrew Simon and Michele Ballet, both of whom conscientiously read and commented on the first draft of the manuscript.

Sheri W. Sussman, my editor at Springer Publishing Company, has been the epitome of kindness, open-mindedness, and professionalism. I would also like to thank Mary Ann McLaughlin, Alana Stein, and Mimi Flow, also at Springer, for their support. Stanley Wakefield, the agent who recognized the potential contribution of this book, can certainly be considered the "prime mover" in all of this, and I thank him for his guidance and persistence in the earliest of stages. In later stages, my aunt, Edythe Sheinbaum, lovingly and tirelessly put her remarkable proofreading skills to work for me; I thank her for her commitment to excellence.

I am deeply grateful to Ken Eisold for writing the foreword. His generosity of spirit is second only to his stature in the field, and I am honored by his endorsement of my work.

Finally, I would like to thank the group of men and women who must remain nameless but without whom there would have been nothing to write—my clients. My clients have been my perpetual inspiration, and I feel fortunate, indeed, to have been allowed to enter their worlds and entrusted with what has often been their most intimate feelings and thoughts. I am especially grateful to those clients who so willingly and enthusiastically allowed me to share their experiences in the case histories that appear in this book.

MULTIDIMENSIONAL
EXECUTIVE COACHING

PART I

Multidimensional Executive Coaching: Foundations

It is the very success of a developing profession that brings on demands for inquiry of that profession.

—Chris Argyris (1975)

CHAPTER 1

Multidimensional Executive Coaching in Action: The Case of Margaret[1]

As I drove through the heavy iron gates and started up the long, curving driveway, I felt a sense of excited anticipation. I was about to meet a new client—a prominent researcher who had the potential of influencing national policy in her area. She had recently been promoted to head a high-profile unit in the highly regarded research division of a well-known corporation in the Northeast. The initial request to meet with her had come from her supervising manager, Steve, the president of the division, with whom I had previously worked. "She needs your help," he had said. Then he added, "And she will probably prove to be the most intellectually stimulating of all your assignments."

I entered the main building, a renovated mansion on an estate that had been converted to the research division's headquarters. I followed the directions she had given me to her office. After several wrong turns, I came across a group of cubicles. They were occupied by women with their heads down, so I politely interrupted the work of one to ask where I could find Margaret's office. Without raising her head, she pointed to the back. The glass door was closed and I knocked. Margaret motioned me in, and I smiled and introduced myself. She readily returned the smile and invited me to sit in one of the chairs facing where she sat behind her desk. There were boxes and piles of paper throughout the room. Her desk was covered with paper.

As I walked to the chair, I was struck by a feeling of great relief. In that moment, I realized that while wandering the mansion's halls for what seemed like an interminably long time, I had had a growing sense of being a character in a gothic novel about to stumble upon some dark secret in a hidden passageway. When I had

[1] The only changes in this case are those made for the purpose of ensuring the confidentiality of the client and the client's organization.

3

at last found the correct area, its somber, impassive inhabitants, and Margaret in her cluttered office, it was as if she were hidden in the attic, grateful that someone had come to rescue her.

As soon as I sat, she said, "I am so happy you are here. I can't believe that someone is going to help me." She then said she felt completely overwhelmed. She described the unit and her work in detail and talked at length about her concerns. The first was the organization of the unit. She was eager to structure it in the way that was "most sensible to operate" but did not know what that was. Its current structure had evolved as the result of an interpersonal conflict between the two people who reported directly to her: her administrative manager, Veronica, and her research manager, Brian. She described Brian as a "no-nonsense" person who got things done and was highly effective running multiple projects, and Veronica as a highly talented but temperamental administrator. She explained that her relationship with Veronica had greatly deteriorated and handed me a letter that Veronica had recently written, enumerating her frustrations with Margaret and the unit.

I took a few moments to read the letter and was shocked by its belligerent and condescending tone. "Have you addressed any of these issues with her?" I asked. "No, she is just so angry at me," Margaret said apologetically.

Before I could ask her for more detail, she turned to another concern. She told me that she had believed that being housed in the main research building, thereby having to rely on the divisional infrastructure, had been a great disadvantage because of her relationship with the former vice president of research, Joseph, who had been in his position for 12 years. Now that he had been promoted to executive vice president and was in a different location, she was more optimistic. She described herself as being "afraid" of Joseph because he was always angry at her. When I asked her what he was angry about, she shuddered and said, "I don't know. Everything."

Margaret next informed me that she and the current research vice president already had a strong bond as the only biologists in the interdisciplinary research division and the only women on the senior management team. She was hopeful that their alliance would aid her in overcoming both the rigidity of divisional administration and the misgivings of her peers, physicians and neuropsychologists uncertain of the value of her new unit. She believed that if she could ameliorate these tensions, her unit would figure prominently in the growing prestige of the division. She reported that, in addition to her position as unit director, she taught two advanced seminars at an affiliated medical school.

The fact that she now had little time to engage in her own research was a source of considerable frustration, although Steve had told her that the unit would be her research laboratory. She stated that her goals for the coaching were to organize the unit appropriately, to develop her organizational leadership skills (including motivation, delegation, and "administrative savvy"), and to carve out time for strategic work.

She listened attentively to my explanation of the coaching process. When I gave her the choice of waiting for the results of feedback interviews that would provide a composite of how she was perceived or, in view of her objectives, beginning the one-on-one coaching simultaneously, she reiterated her desire to start work immediately. Consequently, we agreed that an initial objectives-setting session with Steve would be helpful.

As I left the building, I realized how much I already liked Margaret. She was warm and engaging, and I was impressed with how open and willing to ask for help she had been. There was not the slightest bit of pretentiousness nor arrogance about her. As a result, I found her evident disorganization somewhat endearing. I was, however, quite perplexed by her fear of others' anger, which had the effect of transforming a self-reliant and accomplished professional into a bewildered and vulnerable innocent. It appeared to make no sense given her reputation and stature not only within the company but in the industry at large.

Steve was the first to speak at the meeting. He stated that he wanted Margaret to be an effective, efficient, and happy manager. He explained that he hoped she could become comfortable with directing and planning research rather than doing it herself and that, to do so, she needed to delegate and utilize people better. He told her that she had the reputation of being an "emotional" manager and emphasized that she needed to learn how to get the best from imperfect people—like Veronica and even Joseph. As soon as Steve mentioned Joseph, Margaret's relaxed attentiveness vanished. She leaned forward, her face flushed. "Are you saying that you think I am at fault for the problems with Joseph? Is that why Ruth is working with me?" she demanded. Steve, slightly taken aback but without changing his tone, explained that this was not the case, but that he had been concerned she would perceive it that way and had thought about having another coach work with Joseph. That calmed Margaret, and Steve continued. He stated that he hoped Margaret would learn how to do more "behind the scenes politicking" in order to make things happen. At that point, Margaret became visibly angry. She informed Steve that she was extremely savvy politically and recounted the many ways in which she had gotten things done in the division by utilizing that savvy. Steve looked stunned. "I had no idea," he stammered. "I apologize. Please accept my belated gratitude for your heretofore unrecognized contributions."

As Margaret and I left, she asked me if she had been too forceful. I told her that I did not believe she had done any damage to herself and, in fact, probably had heightened Steve's respect for her. She then told me that she believed Joseph had intentionally withheld the information about her contributions in an attempt to discredit her.

I had seen another side of Margaret in this meeting. I had been surprised by the intensity of her reactions and the degree to which she viewed Joseph as an enemy. I hypothesized that Joseph was the recipient of such strong projections because he represented parts of herself that she did not want to see. I made a mental note to explore that in later meetings. As I soon discovered, however, her responses were caused by circumstances of a very different nature.

When Margaret and I met next, I had conducted more than half of the feedback interviews with her staff and peers. I was therefore equipped to bring a more informed perspective to the issue that Margaret raised—what to do about Veronica. Margaret reported that things were becoming quite unbearable, and that Veronica was affecting the rest of the staff and had publicly announced that she was seeking opportunities elsewhere in the corporation. I asked Margaret if she had confronted Veronica with the unacceptability of her behavior. When she said she had not, I asked why she was allowing Veronica to intimidate her so. Margaret again stated that it was because Veronica was so angry at her.

"Here is the opportunity!" I thought to myself. Aloud I asked, "Margaret, have there been other situations in which you have had a similar reaction?"

"Well, there was this medical student who angrily accused me of being racist and sexist in a seminar I was conducting. It was horrible. It ruined the rest of the seminar for me."

"And has it happened in any other settings?"

Margaret was silent for a moment. "Well, there was my father," she quietly said. She explained that her father had had outbursts of anger throughout her childhood and adolescence. She recounted an incident in which her father had gotten angry at her when she was home for Thanksgiving during her freshman year in college—he had driven her to the airport, paid for a plane ticket back to school, put her on the plane, and had given her no money. When she landed, there was no one to call and no means of transportation. She stated that she was the one who was always blamed for her father's outbursts, so if her brothers or her mother were the recipients of his rage, it was Margaret's fault. As a result, she tried, usually unsuccessfully, not to do anything to anger him. Her escape was to focus on her studies.

Margaret stopped and looked at me in amazement. "I never realized that this was affecting me at work!"

While Margaret was telling me her story, she appeared impassive, relating the details in a composed, perfunctory fashion. I, on the other hand, was having a strong emotional reaction. I felt outraged and protective. When she finished, I said nothing for a few moments. Then, the words came instinctively.

"We can talk about ways in which you might handle what you've just discovered. But this has been a major insight, and, for now, it might be best just to absorb it."

Margaret agreed. I asked if she was all right. She assured me that she was. We arranged to meet again one week later.

I left the building, walked to my car, rested my head on the steering wheel, and cried. As I drove back to my office, I considered that Margaret might wonder whether her disclosure was appropriate. I concluded that it would be an opportune time to review the boundaries between coaching and therapy and to reassure her that what she had shared was entirely acceptable—and safe—within the confines of the coaching relationship.

Margaret plunged directly into a discussion of her need to communicate better when we met the following week. As the entire interview process now was almost complete, I was able to corroborate that this was a perception about her that others also held. We spoke about the need for staff meetings and how to elevate their content as well as the need for clear communication of expectations. Margaret, having thought about it, cited several examples of how her lack of clarity had caused misunderstandings with her staff.

As the meeting neared completion, I readied myself to bring up the previous session. Before I had the opportunity, Margaret did it for me. She informed me that she had been in therapy and had dealt with her family history in relation to her personal life, but that she was astonished that her behavior at work was also affected. I assured her that it would be unusual if it were not, and that it was a courageous and important step for her to tell me about the more painful aspects of her history. "It's like having an elephant in the room," I said. "If we don't know it's there, we'll keep tripping over it. The difference between our work and therapy is that we'll figure out ways to walk around the elephant; therapy is the process to use if you want it out of the room—or at least want to reduce its size." That explanation appeared to make perfect sense to Margaret.

I left the meeting relieved that Margaret was comfortable both with her disclosure and my explanation. I was quite pleased with my analogy, particularly because it had come to me so spontaneously.

When we met again, Margaret announced, "I feel ready to speak with Veronica. I'd like your help in preparing for it." Our meeting centered on the most effective manner in which to confront the unacceptable behaviors and communicate clear expectations while maintaining Veronica's self-esteem. My interviews were now almost completed, and a pattern was emerging regarding the perception of Margaret's strengths and developmental needs. In this case, it seemed particularly appropriate to leverage her strengths, which included her genuineness, her kindness, her ability to listen, and her willingness to set high standards for herself and others. In structuring the discussion, a key factor was the fact that their relationship, when it began, had been productive and mutually supportive. Margaret said she would continue to prepare and asked that I sit in on the discussion. I said I would do so if Veronica gave her consent.

Margaret decided to bring up the topic at the end of her regular weekly meeting with Veronica. I arrived at the beginning of that meeting; Margaret, as we had agreed, explained that I was sitting in for two reasons—to observe her interaction with Veronica and to make certain that Margaret was hearing what Veronica had to say. She asked Veronica if she had any objection, and Veronica indicated that she had already shared many of her concerns with me during the individual interview, so it was fine with her. The first part of the meeting consisted of a status report and calendar update. Veronica took the leadership role. Her tone was authoritative. Margaret then introduced the topic of their relationship. She began by telling Veronica how productive their relationship had been at the beginning and gave her specific examples of what had made it so effective. She then expressed regret that it had deteriorated so badly. She stated that she would support Veronica in her search for a job elsewhere in the company, but while she was still part of the research unit, there were a number of things that were expected of her. Margaret then stated what those expectations were and the ways in which Veronica's current behavior was not acceptable. Margaret was poised, professional, and even throughout. She was firm without being harsh. Veronica sat and listened without saying a word. When Margaret was finished, she asked Veronica how she felt about what had just been said. Veronica burst into tears and left the room. Margaret looked at me for help. I told her that she could not have handled the situation more effectively. A few moments later, Veronica returned and apologized for leaving. She turned to Margaret and talked about how difficult it was to do her job with Margaret so busy and on the road so frequently, how she constantly tried to hold things together and felt as though she failed, and how unappreciated she felt. Her tone was sincere and respectful. Margaret told her how sorry she was to have placed such a burden on Veronica and asked her to think about what support she needed to do her job.

When Veronica left the room, I asked Margaret how she felt about what had just happened. Margaret was pleased. She told me that she had prepared her comments in the same way that she prepared for a professional presentation about her research findings. She had thought about what she wanted to communicate, had organized her thoughts, and had followed the plan. I encouraged her to follow that process any time she planned to have a discussion with an employee, particularly if confronting a difficult subject and especially if she was concerned that the employee might become angry.

As I left Margaret's office, I passed Veronica's desk. I told her how courageous she was for returning to the room and finishing the discussion. "Thank you," she said. "Thank you for everything."

I could not decide who was more pleased with what had transpired—Margaret or I. I was amazed by what I had seen and felt grateful to be engaged in this work.

The following week, Margaret happily reported that there had been a dramatic positive change in Veronica's behavior. She then reported that there had been a spillover to her home environment—she had used the same technique with her teenaged son, and it had been equally effective. She explained that she had been a "dirty fighter" at home, and, although she was willing to admit when she was wrong, she had always suspected that there was a better way. She felt she had now discovered it and wished she had been able to use it when her children were younger. We talked about the relevance of establishing clear boundaries, and the rest of the session was devoted to how she could continue to define and communicate expectations with the rest of her staff.

Because of Margaret's travel schedule, it was 3 weeks before we met again. She reported progress in all areas. The relationship with Veronica had returned to the way it had been at the beginning, she had confronted an issue with a research supervisor, and she was preparing to discuss a problem with Brian. She also had thought through a new organizational structure—one that would give Veronica more support, require Veronica and Brian to collaborate, and provide a link to the divisional infrastructure. She decided to hold her first monthly staff meeting the following week, and we went over the agenda together. She asked me whether I thought it would be a good idea to invite the division staff that supported her group, and I told her that was an excellent idea. Toward the end of the session, she reported that, despite all of this progress, she continued to feel overwhelmed. I suggested that she keep a daily log of all of her activities so that we could identify those tasks that could either be delegated or eliminated. She said she thought that was a great idea and then paused and said, with trepidation in her voice, "But eliminating makes me nervous. Can I eliminate and still be successful?" I reminded her that all she was doing at this stage was attempting to identify the tasks. Making decisions about them would come later—and, even then, she would be the judge of priorities. That appeared to satisfy her.

Once again, I was startled. I would have understood, and even anticipated, a reluctance to eliminate commitments based on Margaret's drive and high standards for achievement. But fear was something quite unexpected. Did she not know that she was considered a superstar in her field and indispensable to the company? Did she not recognize her stature and feel secure about her position? A "need to believe in herself" had come up in the feedback interviews. I had assumed it referred to her decision making; perhaps it also applied here. I noted her reaction (and my own) so that we could return to it at a later time.

Her staff meeting, to which I had been invited, was a huge success. Her presentation of goals was inspirational, her explanation of the new organizational structure was explicit, and her demeanor was engaging and participative. When it concluded, I walked to her office to congratulate her. A group had gathered in the outer office to express how much they had enjoyed and learned from the meeting. Margaret was glowing when I left.

We had postponed the feedback session to wait for an interview with a former supervising manager whose heavy travel schedule had not permitted an earlier meeting with me. When he returned, the interview had to be postponed. Margaret and I decided not to wait any longer. Margaret listened with interest as I described what I had learned about the organizational context, including the research center, the division, and the corporation as a whole. She was fascinated by the varied, and sometimes contradictory, descriptions of her role. She was visibly uncomfortable with the long list of her strengths. When we got to the areas for improvement, none of it was a surprise, as we had already begun to address the most significant areas. It thus served to confirm her objectives.

As the meeting was concluding, she again talked about how overwhelmed she was feeling. I asked if she had kept the log, and she said she had started it but could not continue. I asked if she could isolate anything specific that was making her feel so overburdened. She talked about the pressures of having to please the physicians and the neurosurgeons. I asked her what she thought would happen if she said no to some of the requests they made. She shuddered. Observing her reaction and remembering her purported lack of confidence in herself, I gave her a special assignment in addition to the log—to identify and acknowledge those things about herself of which she was most proud. I also told her that I would send her the written summary of the feedback prior to our next meeting and asked her to review the list of strengths daily as a reminder of the admiration and respect that others had for her. I concluded by saying, "Margaret, you are a 'star'—I heard that over and over again in the interviews. You have already proved yourself. It is all right to turn some things away." She smiled weakly, and I left.

Our next meeting was two weeks later. I had hoped to introduce the subject of positive reinforcement and reward, the only item in the feedback that we had not yet examined in depth. Margaret seemed unusually distracted when I arrived. She did not greet me with her usual warm hello. Instead, she said, "I am still completely overwhelmed!" When I asked her if she had any sense of why, she emphatically stated it was because she had so much to do and had to do all of it well. "So what I'm hearing you say is that you can't say no to anything and that it all has to be A+ effort." She said, with unmistakable defiance in her voice, that that was essentially the case. I asked her why, and she answered, with obvious annoyance, "We went through that last time. I really don't feel as though I am in a position to say no."

This was the first time I was aware of encountering resistance from Margaret. Why, after all of this time, all that she had shared with me, and all that she had been willing to undertake, was this happening now?

I then asked her if she had reviewed the list of strengths. She reacted sharply: "I am really very uncomfortable doing that. I admire humility, and I want to continue to be humble. And I wish you would stop calling me a 'star.'"

I was taken aback by Margaret's words and the passion with which she said them. It took a moment to recover.

"Margaret, what is this all about?" I quietly asked.

Margaret was intense but calm as she responded to my question: "When I was 5 years old, I played in violin competitions. I had to win. I had to be my mother's 'star.' So I won every competition. But my mother also always told me, 'Pride cometh before the fall,' so I wouldn't get arrogant about my winning. I always felt like such a bad person because I could never be anyone's friend; they were my competitors, and I had to beat them. I have heard 'Pride cometh before the fall' my whole life. Any time things have gone really well and then something awful happened, I felt that it was my punishment." Margaret talked about how she discovered herself at 15, when she spent a summer away from home studying music, and realized that she was not as talented as many others. Being there had shown her a different life, and it had had a strong impact. "My mother brought me up to be a 'Boston Brahmin,'" she continued. "As soon as I could, I left home and moved to Southern California. I married a Silicon Valley executive, started giving dinner parties, had my children, and one day woke up and realized I was a Californian 'Boston Brahmin.' I got divorced and went back to school. Those were hard years as a single parent and a full-time student, but I did it. I had this really nice boyfriend for a while. He jilted me, and I was crushed … I kept thinking, 'Pride cometh before the fall.'" She was then silent, appearing to be lost in thought.

As Margaret had spoken, I found it increasingly more difficult to fight my tears. My mother had been a child prodigy who had renounced the piano when she was 14 because she hated to perform. I grew up hearing about those painful years from my mother and my grandmother. My nephew had just turned four, and I imagined him sitting at a piano, his little fingers at the keys hour after hour. I imagined Margaret as a child, having to win. I felt as though my heart were breaking for her.

After several minutes, she looked at me and said that even though she knew that her mother had made many mistakes, she believed her mother tried her best.

I realized Margaret had had enough, so I said that most parents try to do what they think is best, but sometimes they cannot tell the difference between what is right for them and what is right for their children. What was important for our work was to discover the ways in which these experiences were inhibiting her from being effective professionally. I suggested that we end the session and that she think about it until the next time we met. I checked to see that she was as composed as she appeared; she was. I reminded her that she could call me if she needed me, and I left.

Once again, I got to my car, put my head on the steering wheel, and allowed my tears to flow for her. She had been through so much in her life, had overcome so much, and I was concerned that I had pushed her too far too fast. I felt inadequate to deal with these issues, and I wondered if I should recommend that she reenter therapy before continuing with our work.

I came to the next meeting with some trepidation. I was prepared to make the recommendation that she return to therapy. When I arrived, she greeted me cordially. Before I could say anything, she told me that she was preparing to confront an issue with Brian and was confident that she could handle it. She also told me that she had had another staff meeting and was very pleased with the outcome. She had used it as an opportunity to give praise and recognition to her staff and had seen their positive responses. She then reported that she had thought about "the competition issue" and had practiced doing an "adequate" rather than an "exceptional" job at a recent professional convention. She said that it felt good not to have to "perform" and that the reception had been fine.

I was astonished. Margaret had already begun to integrate her painful insight. My admiration and esteem for her was immeasurable.

She paused briefly and then smiled at me as she said, "You called me a 'star.' That was the trigger for what came up. Now that I know that anger, especially male anger, reminds me of my father, and having to perform reminds me of my mother, I can deal with it."

I said to Margaret, "You are a remarkable person." She smiled warmly. There was nothing more to say. We agreed to wait a month before the next session.

I left convinced that we had reached our objectives; at this point, Margaret needed only reinforcement.

The next session revealed some of the old behavior patterns. Margaret was irritated with Brian but had not spoken to him because she was afraid he would quit. In addition, Margaret was again feeling overburdened. After some brief discussion, Margaret decided to resolve the difficulty with Brian by affirming her great confidence in him and then explaining that there was just one area in which he could improve his performance. She also decided to meet with the heads of the other research departments to discuss priorities and necessary resources. She was confident about her ability to have all of these conversations, and we agreed to wait another month.

Margaret began that session by reporting that she was beginning to feel overwhelmed again. This time, it was because she felt that she did not have anyone to whom to delegate the more complex aspects of the biological research. In addition, her husband was urging her to stop working so hard on weekends and engage in more leisure activities with him. I asked her if it was likely that she would keep the current research staff intact, and she responded with an emphatic yes. I then asked what her alternatives were. She thought for a moment and announced that she did have money in her budget but that she had been hoarding it because she was worried about possible budget cuts. She took a deep breath and added, "But perhaps now is the time to stop acting toward the unit the way I operated struggling through graduate school as a single parent with young children." She determined that she would hire more people with expertise in the required area. I congratulated her. Aside from this matter, she felt that everything else was under control, including her ability to choose when and how to deal with employee issues as they arose. As the meeting drew to a close, I told Margaret that it sounded as if our work were done. She panicked and pleaded for one more session. I told her I did not really think she needed it but that I would be happy to have another session. We agree to wait 2 months before meeting, unless she had the need to speak to me sooner.

When I arrived at our final session, Margaret said she was pleased to see me but did not have anything to talk about. I told her how delighted I was to hear that. She told me that she had gained an enormous amount from the coaching, had a unit that was operating well with happy people in it, and was still busy but no longer overwhelmed. She said she had learned how important it is to establish clear expectations with people and communicate when the expectations were not being met—both with her own staff and with colleagues. She also said she had never understood the importance of recognition for others until now. Finally, she said she realized that when people are angry, it may not be directed against her—maybe not even in the case of her father's anger—and while it would always be hard for her, she could now deal with it more effectively. The only question she had was whether we should meet with Steve to find out if he felt that the objectives had been met. I told her we could certainly do that, but it was my understanding that he had already indicated to her that he saw the positive changes. She agreed that he had repeatedly demonstrated his growing confidence in her, so she did not think it was necessary for that purpose but explained that what she really wanted to do was make sure that she was counteracting all the negative things she was certain Joseph was continuing to say about her. I asked her why she thought Joseph had such omnipotence, and she responded by saying that Joseph could be president some day and make life miserable for her. "Margaret, I think it's time for you to invite Joseph out to lunch and make peace with him," I said. She recoiled and told me she was not ready to do that. I told her that if she wasn't ready, that was all right, but it was the one remaining thing that needed to be confronted. She said that she would do it in time, but not yet. "Think of it as your last homework assignment with a due date that is self-imposed," I said. She nodded and smiled, and I smiled back.

I told her how much I had enjoyed working with her and that she could feel free to call me if she needed me—and that doing so did not mean she was failing. She thanked me, and we said good-bye.

As I left, I thought about how much she had accomplished, how privileged I felt to be a part of her process, and how much I would miss her.

This dramatic and compelling case exemplifies the executive coaching process presented in this book. To the uninitiated, there will be a temptation to explain the change in Margaret simplistically: Two insights about the impact of her childhood experience caused her to reassess her circumstances at work and enabled her to change her behavior. While not incorrect, such an analysis stays at only the most superficial of levels[2] and fails to recognize the central themes inherent in the case:

1. That executive coaching is a complex and demanding process encompassing multidimensional interrelationships among the client, the client's organization, and the consultant.
2. That there must be a reliable methodological framework within which to do the work of executive coaching.
3. That the executive coaching methodology must be guided by theory comprising not only individuals but also organizations and groups.
4. That the consultant doing executive coaching must have (a) training and expertise in management, organizational psychology, and individual psychology; (b) a full knowledge of ethical standards and guidelines related to the field; and (c) the demonstrated capacity to engage in self-scrutiny and self-reflection.

These are also the central themes of this book. They will appear repeatedly in the chapters that follow.

---

[2] The full case analysis is the content of the last chapter of this book, presented there as an encapsulation of all the material that precedes it.

ways that the environment may be supporting the conditions underlying the individual's seemingly maladaptive response. (pp. 88–89)

Tobias thus makes evident the inextricable overlap between consulting to the individual and consulting to the organization. In doing so, he creates an opening for a body of knowledge that, although virtually absent from the current literature, can rightfully be called a direct antecedent. It encompasses theory and practice that come not from psychotherapy, the apparent conceptual precursor in the literature, but from the social-systems thinking inherent in organizational psychology. Within this discipline, three classic research projects exemplify its legacy to contemporary coaching methodology.

ANTECEDENT LITERATURE

The Tremont Hotel Project

The Tremont Hotel Project (Whyte & Hamilton, 1965) was a system-wide intervention within the hotel industry that transpired from 1946 to 1947. The researchers began the project at the behest of the hotel's general manager, who was interested in understanding the role of human relations and the personnel function. Making extensive use of interviewing and observation techniques, the researchers analyzed the problems of the organization from multiple levels—group, intergroup, and individual. Subsequent interventions into every department in the hotel focused on groups as the central unit. At the conclusion of the first year, the team had accomplished six objectives: (1) a new role for personnel function that included enhanced human relations; (2) improvement in the quality of interpersonal relations; (3) reduced labor turnover and increased safety; (4) the development of managers and supervisors, particularly in relation to leadership in group meetings; (5) the perception of improved efficiency and productivity; and (6) the transfer of the initiative to the personnel function. The fact that the contract was not renewed was attributed to the team's failure to address one of the most critical aspects of the organizational problems—the individual leadership behavior of the senior manager. Whyte retrospectively realized that he had not addressed the issue directly because of his own timidity and his ego involvement in continuing the project. Once the project was discontinued, however, Whyte reacted differently, and he was startled by the result:

> Having nothing to gain through holding anything back, I decided to build a main part of the report on our analysis of Smith's leadership style.... I presented him with the ten points used in analyzing his behavior.... Smith was so eager to get it that he locked himself in his office immediately and read

it straight through. When he called me in, it was to express enthusiasm, particularly for my analysis of his own executive behavior. Later, he called his management group together ... [and told them] I had pointed out that he was the main personnel problem of the hotel, and that he intended to profit from the criticisms I had made.

This response left me in a somewhat dazed condition.... I should have taken the initiative much earlier, and confronted him in discussion with our view of his leadership behavior and of its impact upon the organization. (pp. 177–178)

The study's ultimate conclusion regarding Smith is one that has great relevance to executive coaching as we know it today—that changes in the organization and changes in key individuals are inextricably linked.

The Claypool Furniture and Appliances Study

The study at Claypool Furniture and Appliances (Levinson, Molinari, & Spohn, 1972) took place in 1970 at the request of its president, Robert Claypool III, who was interested in the application of motivational concepts in order to strengthen the organization for expansion and to reverse recent profit declines. The researchers used a four-step process: questionnaire completion, interviewing and observation, data analysis and interpretation, and reporting. The gathering of extensive data about the organization through the completion of the questionnaires by 96% of the employees, and individual interviews and observations of the work process with 100 employees randomly selected among those representing seven diverse criteria revealed a number of problems within the company: lack of self-respect in employees, a thwarted desire to participate in decision making, lack of feedback, lack of recognition, salary issues, lack of training, intergroup conflict, lack of formal lines of communication. It also revealed a problem within its leader: Claypool was ambivalent about his role as a paternalistic father figure in the tradition of his grandfather, the founder of Claypool, and his desire to be a competent executive concerned with the performance of the business. The researchers made a number of recommendations regarding improved practices but reached a single conclusion: "The prognosis for the organization hinges on the resolution of Robert Claypool's ambivalence" (p. 489). Their recommended process for helping him do so entailed individual consultations to Claypool and his executive vice president, in which the former could increase his skills in delegation, learn to allow others to make decisions and encourage group problem solving, and the latter, through a "therapeutic alliance" with the consultant, could learn to ease demands on himself, provide guidance and support to his subordinates, and improve his listening skills. These researchers, two decades before executive coaching became popular, had discovered its concurrent individual and systemic value, and they had begun to perform the function.

The Gaight School Study

The Gaight School Study (Alderfer & Brown, 1975) resulted from a 4-year research and consultation project with an exclusive preparatory school for boys. It began in 1969, at the request of the school's headmaster, as a result of the turbulence that the school had experienced the previous academic year. Using a diagnostic process that consisted of the design and implementation of a questionnaire and extensive interviews with groups and individuals, the researchers discovered a number of factors that were affecting the quality of life at Gaight—student harassment, sarcasm as a norm, intergroup conflict, and the ineffectiveness of a group (the prefects) critical to the well-being of the school. The researchers reported their findings and their recommendations in a series of feedback meetings to all groups within the school, noting the microcosm effect of each group's reaction. There were three recommendations: the development of a team of internal consultants to assist with the change process, training for the prefects and an examination of their role, and consultation on decision making. All recommendations were implemented. The first took the form of formal training and ongoing consultation to the members of the staff chosen to be the internal consultants; the second, a consultation to the prefects using group-level analyses and interventions; the third, an individual consultation to the headmaster. Reflecting on the latter, the researcher wrote the following:

> The process of the consultation was nondirective. I neither proposed the problems to be discussed nor offered solutions. I did not attempt to increase the options that were considered and tried to identify factors (often emotional) that the decision makers might have been overlooking. Our working arrangement left the decision about who to include in the sessions to the Headmaster, although we sometimes jointly discussed the possibilities. (p. 144)

One of the internal consultants reported on the consultation from the headmaster's perspective:

> The headmaster is particularly enthusiastic about these sessions. He feels that the airing of tensions and conflicts in the presence of a third party made his job easier in that the energy used to suppress irritations and conflict was now released for other purposes. He firmly believes he could not have led in the initiation of co-education and term-contained courses at Gaight without these sessions and the help of Professor Alderfer. (p. 222)

At the conclusion of the project, the researchers developed a new theory of consultation based on six propositions: (1) that it involves a joint process of inquiry by the client and the consultant; (2) that valid data from the inquiry are contingent upon the mutuality of the relationship and the degree to which boundaries, both physical and psychological, are made permeable, not only between but also within both the client and the consultant; (3) that understanding of the consequences of behavior necessitates both feelings and intellect; (4) that sustained change can occur only when (a) the client chooses to alter behavior, (b) there is a psychological acceptance of the change by all relevant groups and individuals, and (c) the new behavior pattern becomes routine; (5) that two types of interventions are required—"releasing interventions" that facilitate the expressions of suppressed emotion and "developmental interventions" that plan for change; and (6) that consultation consists of four iterative phases: entry and contract agreements, data collection and diagnosis, implementation, and evaluation.

This theory of consultation to organizations, emphasizing considerable emotional, intellectual, and behavioral involvement by the client and the consultant, as well as participation by those individuals and groups most impacted by the potential change, was also clearly applicable to consulting done with individuals when viewed within the full complexity of the organizational context. The relevance to contemporary thought concerning executive coaching is unmistakable, and its influence on the theoretical foundation for this book, as becomes clear in the next chapter, invaluable.

ANNOTATED BIBLIOGRAPHY[2]

Alderfer, C. P., & Brown, L. D. (1975). *Learning from changing: Organizational diagnosis and development.* Beverly Hills, CA: Sage; Levinson, H., Molinari, J., & Spohn, A. G. (1972). *Organizational diagnosis.* Cambridge, MA: Harvard University Press; Whyte, W. F., & Hamilton, E. L. (1965). *Action research for management: A case report on research and action in industry.* Homewood, IL: Richard D. Irwin.

The three works that are not only the forerunners to what is currently considered executive coaching but also the exemplars of the utilization of qualitative methodology. They provide a wealth of information about organizational consultation and the multiple levels that are impacted whenever there is entry into any system.

---

[2] These bibliographies are intended to provide readers with resources that will either deepen or broaden the material presented in each chapter. Several of the works listed also appear in the bibliographies of later chapters; when this is the case, the relevant content is specified.

Kampa-Kokesch, S., & Anderson, M. Z. (2001). Executive coaching: A comprehensive review of the literature. *Consulting Psychology Journal, 53*(4), 205–228.

The most extensive review, to date, of the psychological literature about executive coaching.

Stober, D. R., & Grant, A.M. (Eds.). (2006). *Evidence based coaching: Putting best practices to work for your clients.* Hoboken, NJ: John Wiley & Sons.

A recently published book which, in addition to a wide range of coaching perspectives, contains a comprehensive bibliography of executive coaching articles published in the scholarly literature between 1955 and 2005.

therapeutic relationship to include the reenactment of the original relationship and the substitution of appropriate parental responses (i.e., empathy, mirroring, setting of boundaries, etc.) for the inadequate ones that are the source of the client's difficulties (McWilliams, 1994; Mitchell & Black, 1995).

The transition from depth psychology to the interpersonal and object relations schools represented a change from a one-person to a two-person psychology (Ghent, 1989) and thus expanded the focus from the intrapsychic to include the interpersonal. This focus was further expanded to include the collective when Wilfred R. Bion introduced group-as-whole theory (1961). Bion saw group dynamics as the interplay between individual needs and group mentality and culture. The interplay, he felt, creates a fundamental unconscious conflict between the group mentality and the desires of the individual. This basic conflict is actually composed of two conflicts: the more obvious one between the individual and the group, and the less obvious one between the individual and the self as an upholder of the group. The conflicts produce intrapsychic anxieties that manifest themselves in shared unconscious fantasies ("basic assumptions") on a group level regarding the reason that the group has formed—to obtain security (dependency), to give birth to a "savior" (pairing), to preserve itself from an outside enemy (fight/flight). Individuals in the group, through "valency," demonstrate the extent to which they are willing to combine with the regressed group by "holding" a particular aspect of the basic assumption behavior and unconsciously accepting specific roles on behalf of the group. The work group and the individuals constituting it who come together to accomplish a particular task are thus powerfully, albeit unconsciously, influenced by the primitive regression inherent in basic assumption behavior in the group as a whole.

MULTILEVEL FORCES

As Levinson indicates, organizations also have a psychological side. They are not, however, monoliths. Like all living entities, organizations must define themselves, psychologically as well as physically, through interaction with their environment. In addition, they are not simply influenced by individuals interacting with one another singly or collectively, but also by groups in constant interaction with other groups. Two theories by Clayton P. Alderfer provide further explication.

In his first, the theory of underbounded and overbounded organizations, Alderfer (1980a) provides a vehicle with which to determine the relative boundary permeability of an organization and the resultant prognosis regarding the organization's ability to survive. He describes 11 indicators of boundary permeability—goals, authority, economic conditions, role definitions, communication patterns, human energy, emotional state, intergroup dynamics, unconscious basic assumptions, time span, and prevailing ideology. By observing the nature of these indicators, which are often easier to recognize than the actual boundaries, it is possible to determine whether the organization is overbounded and in danger of losing the ability to interact with its environment or underbounded and subject to being submerged into its outer environment. Overbounded organizations are characterized by explicit goals and priorities, unilateral authority, lack of stress regarding economic conditions, blocked communications, constrained energy, negativity directed outside, dominance of organizational groups, unconscious dependency, long time spans, and singular ideologies. Underbounded systems reveal themselves through the existence of ambiguous goals, competing authority, economic crises, imprecise roles, unclear communication channels, diffuse energy, negativity within and without, dominance of identity groups, fight/flight reactions, short time spans, and multiple ideologies. Furthermore, because of the interdependence of an organization's related subsystems, these indicators can also serve as a vehicle with which to formulate hypotheses regarding the state of the organization's psychological boundaries.

Embedded intergroup relations theory (Alderfer, 1986) not only recognizes the impact of groups within an organization, but also views them as central to an understanding of organizational dynamics at all levels. Alderfer describes five characteristics of intergroup relations—group boundaries (permeability), power differences (accessibility of resources), affective patterns (degree of polarization and projection), cognitive formations (development of theories and ideologies), and leadership behavior (as representative of the total pattern)—and divides groups in organizations into two categories—identity groups, those sharing a common world view (i.e., race, ethnicity, generation, family), and organizational groups, those sharing a common organizational view (i.e., task, hierarchical position). He postulates that any interaction between two individuals must be viewed as an unconscious interaction between the salient identity and/or organizational group memberships of each within the context of a particular social system. Because of this embeddedness, moreover, the relationship among individuals or groups (the subsystems) is shaped by relationships in the larger context (the suprasystem). To this phenomenon, Alderfer assigns the term "parallel process" and demonstrates how observing individuals and groups can give crucial data about dynamics at a broader level. He also demonstrates that embedded intergroup relations and the enactment of parallel processes apply equally to the researcher in interaction with the individual, group, or entire system under study. Hence, by superimposing on Levinson's conception of role formulation the views of analytical psychology, the interpersonal and object relations schools, group-as-whole theory,

embedded intergroup relations theory, and boundary theory, individual performance in organizations becomes a function of the interaction between the
salient conscious and unconscious responses that are triggered in the individual by, respectively and collectively: internal, intrapsychic forces; interactions with other individuals; requirements as a subsystem of a group, acting
on behalf of group life needs; membership in an organizational and/or identity
group in interaction with representatives of the same or other organizational
and/or identity groups; and requirements as an organizational member, all of
which have both conscious and unconscious elements.

USE OF SELF

The consultant, in entering the organization to work with the individual, thus
stands at the intersection of their interaction and, concomitantly, the intersection of multilevel conscious and unconscious forces, including those that the
consultant himself/herself brings as part of his/her being. For the time he/she
is present, the consultant becomes part of the multidimensional system, both
influencing it and being influenced by it. To do the work of executive coaching, then, the consultant must be able to tolerate, and ultimately make use
of, entering a highly complex place—a place that is occupied by neither the
individual nor the organization alone but, because of their convergence, both
the individual and the organization together; a place that contains both the
exigencies of working life and the impulses of the psyche; and a place that
engages and, in turn, is engaged by the consultant's own intrapsychic material. In addition, if the work is done effectively, it requires that the consultant
be both involved enough in the dynamics so as to experience their impact and
detached enough so as to analyze what is transpiring. These demands make
imperative the use of oneself as tool.

The concept of the use of self is pervasive in the foundational theoretical
material that has been discussed thus far. The countertransference—what is
being evoked in the psychologist when working with the client—is viewed
as the cornerstone of the therapeutic process in analytical psychology, in
interpersonal psychology, and in the object-relations school. Parallel processes—unconscious reenactment within the subsystem of suprasystem
dynamics—are a key component in embedded intergroup relations theory. Whether in the language of psychodynamic theory or organizational
theory, however, the message is the same: The consultant must engage
in a continuous process of self-scrutiny in order to identify what is being
evoked in himself/herself so as to appropriately inform his/her choices in
the ongoing process.

David N. Berg and Kenwyn K. Smith (1985) are among the researchers who view self-scrutiny as indispensable to effective work. They point out that it is only through continuous commitment to engage in self-reflection that the researcher can uncover the internal intellectual and emotional forces that impact his/her research. In addition, it is self-examination that makes possible the garnering of information about the dynamics of an individual or a social system through analysis of the countertransference or parallel processes. They also speak to the necessity for self-scrutiny to address the complexities arising from the simultaneous influences on one another of the researcher and those being studied. Cammann (1985) places the same concepts within a consulting context and discusses the need for self-knowledge to counteract the inevitable distortions caused by the consultant's individual preferences and biases in organizational diagnosis, to differentiate between personal and systemic causes of personal reactions in gathering data by direct experience, to recognize the consequences of one's actions in designing interventions, and to recognize projections when encountering resistance.

The same principles apply to executive coaching. To work in this manner, however, places a number of demands on the consultant. It requires that the consultant bring with him/her a thorough knowledge of his/her own biases, experiences, characteristic responses, and group memberships. It requires that the consultant be willing to engage in continuous self-reflection throughout the process to determine what thoughts and emotions are being evoked and to differentiate between characteristic responses and those triggered by the current circumstances. It requires that the consultant use what is evoked in him/her to formulate and test hypotheses about the unconscious multilevel forces impacting the individual with whom he/she is working. It requires that the consultant use his/her own thoughts and emotions to inform the selection and implementation of the appropriate interventions for both the individual and the organization, maintaining a keen awareness that (a) any intervention with the individual is a simultaneous intervention with the organization, and that (b) any change in the individual must be supported by the organization, thereby implying that the organization must be prepared to ultimately support a change in itself.

In this context, the consultant uses himself/herself as the tool with which to gain, through direct experience, an empathetic understanding of the following:

- The inner life of the individual being coached and the specific intrapsychic forces that are being triggered by other individuals, groups, intergroup relations in the organization, and organizational role demands.
- The characteristic interpersonal patterns of the individual being coached and of other individuals with whom the individual is in contact.

- The impact of and reaction to one's own group memberships, and consequently, the nature of the organization's embedded intergroup relations.
- As a result of repeated entry, the relative boundary permeability of the organization, its attendant psychological boundaries, and the nature of work life within the organization.
- The impact of the consultant's ongoing interventions on both the individual and the organization.

Translating this understanding into words and actions that are meaningful to the client is what the practice of executive coaching is about. The chapters that follow demonstrate how it is accomplished.

ANNOTATED BIBLIOGRAPHY

Alderfer, C. P. (1986). An intergroup perspective on group dynamics. In J. Lorsch (Ed.), *Handbook of organizational behavior* (pp. 190–222). Englewood Cliffs, NJ: Prentice Hall.
The seminal article on unconscious intergroup dynamics, organizational embeddedness, and parallel processes, no consultant should venture forth without reading this article several times. (Once is not enough to capture its depth and comprehensiveness.)
Berg, D. N. & Smith, K. K. (Eds.) (1985). *Exploring clinical methods for social research.* Beverly Hills, CA: Sage.
A compendium of works in the tradition of which multidimensional coaching is a part, containing several excellent chapters on the use of self as a tool.
Bion, W. R. (1961). *Experiences in groups.* New York: Basic Books.
In the category of seminal works, this is the one for unconscious intergroup dynamics.
Campbell, J. (Ed.). (1971). *The portable Jung* (R. F. C. Hull, Trans.). New York: Penguin Books.
For those understandably unnerved by the formidable undertaking of reading *The Collected Works,* this book is an excellent introduction.
Jung, C. G. (1989). *Memories, dreams, reflections* (A. Jaffe, Ed., R. Winston & C. Winston, Trans.). New York: Vintage Books. (Original work published 1962)
An autobiography of the icon, this book traces not only Jung's life but also the development of his theoretical thought and his therapeutic approach.
Levinson, D. J. (1959). Role, personality and social structure in the organizational setting. *Journal of Abnormal & Social Psychology, 58,* 170–180.
Yet another seminal piece, this article was the first serious treatise on organization role and the first to consider it from a psychoanalytic perspective.

McWilliams, N. (1994). *Psychoanalytic diagnosis.* New York: Guildford Press.
A thorough, very readable book on character patterns from a psychodynamic perspective.
Rice, A. K. (1963). *The enterprise and its environment.* London: Tavistock.
The progenitor of all organizational psychology, this should be in every organizational consultant's personal library.
Westen, D. (1990). Psychoanalytic approaches to personality. In L. Pervin (Ed.), *Handbook of personality theory and research* (pp. 21–63). New York: Guilford.
Excellent overview of the history of psychodynamic personality theory and practice.

Phase I. Entry

Entry generally tells the organization's story very well. As a working heuristic, it is useful to assume that the major dynamics are all observable at entry, if the consultant is able to perceive them.

—Clayton P. Alderfer (1980)

CHAPTER 5

Preliminary Meeting

If the contact person and the consultant agree to proceed, the next step in entry is an on-site meeting between the consultant and the prospective client in the latter's office. The primary purpose of meeting is for each to make an informed decision about whether to work together.

The consultant's responsibility, therefore, is to accomplish the following:

- *Exploring the client's receptivity or resistance to coaching:* This can be done by finding out what the client hopes to gain from coaching, whose idea it was to engage a coach, and how the client, in general, feels about the coaching process.
- *Explaining to the client all aspects of coaching:* The explanation includes the steps in the process, the nature of confidentiality, the differences between coaching and therapy, and the role of the coach.
- *Observing the client's behavior:* The manner in which the client behaves toward the consultant and others while the consultant is present, how the consultant reacts to the client's behavior, and whether the behavior is consistent with what has been previously described are key areas for observation.
- *Determining the comfort level between the client and the consultant:* While the personality traits of the consultant and the client are a factor in establishing a sense of openness and trust, it is the consultant's salient organizational and identity group memberships in relation to those of the client that ultimately determine the strength of the working alliance.
- *Experiencing organizational entry:* What occurs as the consultant physically enters the organization provides valuable information about boundaries, whether there will be the right degree of permeability for the work to be done effectively, and how it feels to be a part, albeit temporarily, of the organization. It also provides data with which to refute, confirm, or modify the initial hypotheses.

Excerpts from three cases—the first two a continuation from the last chapter, the third a particularly vivid illustration—provide examples of the value and power of the preliminary meeting.

THE CASE OF HOWARD (continued)

For my first meeting with Howard, I entered the high-rise office building and was reminded of the many years I had spent in a similar financial services environment. I was cleared through security and given a visitor's pass, and a telephone call was made to announce my arrival. An attractive young woman who identified herself as Joan, Howard's assistant, came to the lobby to escort me to the elevators and to his office. She was cordial and adept at conversation.

When we got to Howard's office, a sunlit private space with tasteful furniture and a view of the river, Joan introduced me to a tall, well-dressed, middle-aged man with a pleasant expression. He invited me to sit, and Joan offered coffee before she left, closing the door behind her.

Howard asked if the directions had been clear; I told him they were perfect. He then told me that he had read my resume, was very impressed with my background, and had wanted to work with someone who understood management theory and had been a line manager. I asked him if he had any questions about me before we began, and he said he did not. I then asked him why he had requested a coach.

He said that he had had a 360-degree evaluation performed and could not interpret some of the results. He explained, with a sad expression, that he had been at his present company for almost 30 years and had never been in a situation like the present one. When I asked him to describe what that was, he said that he had a new manager, a woman in her early thirties from outside the division, who appeared to be very dissatisfied with his performance. I asked him how he knew that, and he showed me a copy of the 360 results and added that she was abrupt with him and critical of his work. He said that he felt it necessary to check with her on every decision he made and, as a result, was second-guessing himself and feeling paralyzed much of the time.

As he handed me the report, my mind flashed back 15 years. I had been in a similar situation, and my anger and frustration with the situation felt palpable. I reminded myself to stay in the moment and not to jump to premature conclusions.

When I glanced at the report, I realized that his manager's evaluation was, in fact, quite different from those of his direct reports and his peers. In addition, her ratings were lowest in those areas that the organization deemed critical skills. I told Howard that I would like to have some time to review the results in detail, but that, indeed, his manager's ratings seemed unusual when compared with others. I also told him that I felt comfortable working with him and that if he felt the same, we could "officially" begin at the next session. He agreed and we set a date to meet. He escorted me to the elevator. (I was permitted to return to the lobby on my own.)

I left the building feeling relieved that I had changed careers, angry about his treatment, and determined to help him.

THE CASE OF JEANNE (continued)

For my first meeting with Jeanne, I had been instructed to leave my car in a designated space near the office building. As I entered, I noticed how bright and inviting it was. People were seated in the lobby, and its own café was on the entry-level floor. I took the elevator to Jeanne's office and found it easily. As soon as I entered, she greeted me pleasantly but with a rather clipped formality, came from around her desk to shake my hand, and inquired about my parking. Jeanne was small in stature, appeared to be in her mid-thirties, and was well dressed. She gave me a parking pass and advised me to return to my car so that I would not be towed (I learned later that building maintenance was one of her many responsibilities). When I returned, she sat beside me in one of two chairs facing her desk and looked at me expectantly. I asked her why I was there. She said there were several reasons—that she felt overwhelmed with work most of the time and needed to learn about time management, that she needed to better handle people whom she was not sure she liked or respected, and that she was having difficulty managing an issue of suspected substance abuse. I asked if she had any sense of why these areas were difficult for her. Her response was unhesitating and forthright. The substance abuse concern, which she viewed as urgent to address, was so difficult because her father was an alcoholic and the suspected substance abuser, Carl, was a close personal friend whose relationship Jeanne was "terrified" of losing. Jeanne's reluctance was compounded by the fact that several people had been fired when she had taken on her role as vice president. Although the decisions had been the president's, Jeanne was seen as the "hatchet person." In one case, a letter about her had been written to an internal newsletter, accusing her of mismanagement and racism. Although it was subsequently shown to be untrue, Jeanne had been hurt and embarrassed by the incident and did not want to do anything that might cause a similar incident.

I described the coaching process to Jeanne and told her that if she wanted to proceed, I would be happy to work with her. She stated that she was comfortable working with me and wanted to start as soon as possible. I suggested that, given the immediacy of the substance abuse issue, we not wait for the completion of feedback interviews to begin work in that area. She concurred, I discussed the confidentiality of all data, and we agreed to meet with the president for a joint goal-setting session. It was arranged for the following week.

I left her office admiring her ability to be so open and trusting. I felt competent and in control with a strong sense of obligation to help her.

THE CASE OF MARY

I was escorted to Mary's office by her manager, Ann, an elegant woman in her late fifties. Ann, the executive director of the community outreach agency for which Mary was marketing director, had placed the initial call and wanted to meet with me before introducing me to Mary. During that meeting, she told me that Mary was very smart and talented but she had problems with the rest of the staff. They found Mary overbearing and demeaning, with little interest in others' points of view. There had been relatively high turnover in the marketing department, and Ann was concerned that it was as a result of Mary's style. In addition, as Mary had had no formal training in marketing and I had strong prior experience in the area, Ann requested that I support her in the development of a marketing plan.

When I entered Mary's office, she stood and came from around her desk to greet me. She was in her early forties and dressed in the comfortable, casual manner that appeared to be the norm for the agency. The office was small but pleasant, and there were neat piles of paper on the desk, bookshelves, and round table at which Mary and I sat. She moved aside a pile to make room for me to write.

When I smiled at her, she returned the smile, but I detected a guardedness in her expression. I asked her why, from her perspective, I was there. "I'm not really sure," she said. "I think it's to help me create an effective marketing function within the organization." She stopped momentarily, then added, looking carefully at my face, "And Ann is under the impression that people are afraid of me."

"What do you think about that?" I asked her, without averting my eyes.

She responded that she thought that was really not true. As Mary saw it, the issue was that people did not understand her role and that they got upset because they thought she was involved in areas that were their domain. "If they understood the role of marketing, then they would recognize what I'm trying to do. The problem is that I'm very direct and to the point, and people here don't know how to be direct."

"That must be Jeanne," Bob said. "Come right in," he called.

When Jeanne joined us at the conference table, they both looked at me expectantly. I summarized the purpose of the meeting—to make certain that we all agreed on the goals for coaching—and then intentionally stopped speaking. Bob spoke first, repeating what he had told me in our first telephone conversation—that Jeanne needed to improve her interpersonal relationships and that it was imperative that she confront the substance abuse issue. He also emphasized the desirability of her learning to control her tendency to become overwhelmed. Despite Jeanne's presence at the conference table, he spoke about her in the third person. At the conclusion of his comments, however, he turned to her, smiled warmly, and said in a tone that was more parental than supervisory, "Jeanne, you have to learn to say no, even to me." Jeanne nodded her agreement but remained respectfully silent.

Throughout the meeting, I had been waiting for the subject of Gail and the document to come up. It did not. Because I did not know if Jeanne knew about it, I did not raise it directly. I intended to subtly encourage Bob to do so.

Before I could do that, Bob stood, announced that he had to rush off to another site, and left the room. After his abrupt departure, I asked Jeanne if she was comfortable with what had been discussed. She stated that she was. She then gave me a typed list of the interviewees she had selected, and we scheduled our next meeting.

I left the building with a sense of confusion and a disturbing distrust of Bob.

ANALYSIS: THE CASES OF HOWARD AND JEANNE

In these two cases, the previously described relationships between the clients and their managers could not have stood in more contradistinction to one another. Yet, the cases were startlingly alike in that each relationship was almost the opposite of what it first appeared to be. By examining each relationship, moreover, the complexities of the unconscious forces in both cases continued to reveal themselves.

In the first case, it was evident at the outset that the manager was in charge—and that the client was not. The manager's expectation that the consultant would begin the meeting—and the client's need to be prompted—was an immediate indicator of the authority dynamics in the room. In addition, the manager's directness, almost to the point of bluntness, disclosed three essential pieces of information. First, the lack of framing or softening demonstrated that she had given little thought to how her comments would affect the client. Second, the manager's strongly favorable position regarding the client had not been discussed previously. The lack of open communication between the manager and the client was therefore quite visible. Third, prevailing organizational dynamics in relation to age and gender were completely reversed in this relationship (i.e., the younger white female, rather than the older white male, was in the dominant role both organizationally and behaviorally).

As a result, a number of previous hypotheses were corroborated. First, there was, indeed, a need for the client to work on the relationship with his manager, and it was one that centered on improved communication. By his taking the initiative in this area, furthermore, he would be demonstrating some of the very skills that his manager perceived were required for further advancement. Second, the consultant's group memberships had been a factor in the meeting. Interestingly, what was most salient here was not age or gender, as initially expected, but professional expertise. The manager had initially deferred to the consultant as the expert and had been willing, on two occasions, to be directed, however subtly, to the client. Third, it was increasingly clear that this was a highly overbounded organization. The authority dynamics were hierarchical—so hierarchical, in fact, that they could supersede age and gender dynamics. This, as well as what emerged as the consultant's salient membership in this setting, indicated the predominance of organizational rather than identity groups. Communication was obviously blocked. Furthermore, the reluctance by the client, a seasoned senior executive, to take the lead not only in the meeting but also in the relationship with his manager indicated an underlying basic assumption of dependency that certainly had to be identified and overcome if he was to progress.

The client demonstrated the determination to overcome the dependency not only by his willingness to take on the responsibility for the relationship with his manager, but also by identifying those aspects of his behavior that he was unwilling to change. The prognosis for a successful coaching outcome was therefore a positive one.

In the second case, the manager had given every indication of being extraordinarily supportive of the client and her desire to change. Yet, his actions in this meeting seemed to contradict the initial data. Whether consciously or unconsciously, he was repeatedly sabotaging the client. His blunder with the document was the clearest example, but there were others: the covert conversation with the consultant, the transparent desire to gain the consultant's sympathy, domination of the conversation, and the tight control of the content and time boundaries of the meeting. All of these things served to silence and disempower the client.

And it was curious that the client seemed to be so willing a partner in this interaction. In the initial meeting, she was honest, forthright, open, articulate and very self-possessed, both personally and professionally. She had initiated

In the second case, the contract was treated perfunctorily—as merely the written confirmation of previous understandings. From the organization's perspective, entry had been accomplished during the initial telephone call, and the consultant was already engaged in the work.

Thus, the initial hypotheses about the nature of boundaries in the respective organizations were confirmed. The contract was a vehicle for final corroboration. It also served another critical purpose: It was the first formal systemic intervention in each organization. In the first case, the contract increased the permeability of organizational boundaries—at least enough to allow entry to occur at all. At the same time, it decreased the permeability of the coaching boundaries—stipulating that further attempts to breach confidentiality would negate the contract. In the second case, the contract established boundaries in an organization that appeared to have few in place. Both interventions were essential for effective work if the clients were, respectively, to risk challenging the rigid hierarchical structure and to define the limits of role and responsibility.

As we move into the next phase of coaching, we leave behind our now familiar cases and turn to others that more vividly illustrate the impact of the next steps in the process. We will, however, revisit several in later chapters.

in high school and achieved through perseverance, practice, and intensity. I was the first in my family to go to college and selected a school based purely on where I could play football. In the second week of practice, I broke my arm in six places and then made a startling discovery: I loved school; I loved to learn; I loved to study. I transferred to a more academically oriented college, and I became an RA so I could have my own room. I met my wife there, we got married as soon as we graduated 23 years ago, and we have three children. I am the 'provider' and have lots of success here. We live in a great place to raise children, they walk to school and are all good students. I broke the family pattern of a long line of policemen and firemen living in urban, blue-collar neighborhoods. My football star cousin is now a Marine colonel. As for sports, I now run marathons."

He then transitioned back to his job. He described the organization as a highly political one in which people were considered disposable and the stakes were very high: "Like playing in the NFL without pads," he offered. One of his concerns was the perception of how closely tied he was to the CFO; his other concerns revolved around perceptions of him personally ("I took the FIRO-B and it showed I have the affiliation needs of a rock"), particularly in this environment in which people were still mourning the loss of colleagues and exhausted from the pace of the work over the course of the previous year.

The interview process brought into sharp focus the environment in which Jim was working and his assessment of others' perceptions of him. The organization was described as "cut-throat," his division as "hatchet people," and the CFO as "reactive and crisis-oriented." There was wide agreement that he was expected to take up multiple roles requiring different, and sometimes mutually exclusive, skill sets, making it almost impossible to do his job well. This made the often contradictory information more understandable: Most identified numerous strengths, which included strategic vision, executional excellence, strong leadership skills, intelligence, and a strong sense of humor. Many also saw him as confident, empowering, motivational, empathetic, and responsive. On the other hand, he was perceived as fearful of mistakes, overly critical, inaccessible, detached, and impatient. The phrase "Good Jim/Bad Jim" characterized a prevalent view of him as unpredictable, inconsistent, and moody.

My own reactions to him remained highly positive throughout the assessment phase. While I was readily able to observe the focus and the intensity, I did not experience the inconsistency and moodiness. I concluded that either he was screening this behavior from me or I was perceiving it differently from the other with whom I had spoken, and that additional data would emerge in later stages.

THE CASE OF STEVEN

On the same day as my first meeting with Steven, the 49-year-old COO of a large nonprofit human services organization, I returned to my office and found an e-mail with the names he had selected for the feedback interviews. There were 27 people listed.

As I reflected upon our meeting earlier in the day, I was not surprised by the length of the list nor the speed with which it had been generated. During our discussion, he had informed me that he was seeking coaching because he had been "fired" from his position as director of the service center that he had managed for the last six years, a job that he had performed concurrently with his work as COO. The "demotion," as he had described it, was a result of what the agency's new CEO described as his "nonparticipatory management style" and his flaws: perfectionism, abruptness, and impatience. "I just don't have time for kidding around, and I don't have a high tolerance for people who ignore simple rules and regulations. My job is to make things run and to problem solve, not to baby-sit a group of professionals who should know better." He had then efficiently and dispassionately enumerated six objectives for coaching: to improve his "people skills" so that he could be a more effective manager; to manage his life better; to enjoy work life more; to exit appropriately from the directorship; to set appropriate goals with people; and to learn anything else that benefited him. He emphasized that he was willing to cooperate in any way, including having me speak with his therapist at any time that might be helpful.

It was 6:30 p.m., so I called Steven expecting to leave a voicemail message. He answered his phone. I told him I had received the e-mail and suggested that he consider reducing the number of people on the interview list. Steven's response was abrupt and accusatory: "But you *told* me to give you the names of people who know me well!" I was startled by his tone but recovered quickly and said firmly, "Yes, and I appreciate your thoroughness, but I believe it would be in everyone's best interest to reduce the number to under twenty." I agreed to meet with him to help him revise the list and planned to do the psychodynamic interview at that time.

We spent about a half-hour on the list. As I prepared to transition to the interview, Steven said he wanted me to know that the next day he intended to tell people at work that he was divorcing his wife. When I asked him how he felt about the divorce, he told me that it was particularly difficult because they had been life-long friends. I asked him if he was discussing the divorce with his therapist. He said he was. I told him that I thought this would be an appropriate time for me to contact her. He readily agreed.

as became apparent at the very next meeting when the client demonstrated a willingness to reveal deeply personal information to the consultant. It was not until the conversation with the client's therapist, however, that the full impact of the intervention became evident: Someone was, perhaps for the first time, performing a responsible parental task for him by setting limits in a supportive and nonjudgmental way. The therapist's information also provided insight into the sources of the client's wounding, the underlying reasons for the current pain, and the causes of dysfunctional behavior. Having grown up in an environment of emotional neglect, he had achieved the only recognition he had known in his professional milieu. His sense of urgency and drive for perfection had been reinforced many times over; now, it was the cause for rejection. Concurrently, his marriage was ending. His attempt to substitute a family, be it personal or organizational, for the one he never had was thus proving futile. His sense of confusion and loss was profound.

The 360-degree interviews revealed that extreme splitting was occurring in reaction to the client. This dichotomy mirrored his own behaviors toward those with whom he worked—he either loved them and was a wonderful friend or he reviled them and made no attempt to disguise his contempt. His outer world had become a reflection of his inner world. Both would have to be addressed in all aspects of the ensuing work.

In the third example, the client's interactions with the consultant stood in stark contrast to those with others closely associated with him. During the psychodynamic interview, he was forthright, discussing his family of origin, his early professional goals, his military career and his divorce with a self-reflective wistfulness that engendered empathy and affection in the consultant. But the 360-degree interviews and the observation of the staff meeting revealed a very different side—one characterized by insensitivity and the need for restrictive control—of which the client seemed to be completely unaware. It was only after gathering the additional data that the consultant realized the degree to which the client consistently minimized distressing experiences as a way to disown his own painful emotions. But it was unclear to her whether the client's lack of awareness was a result of his characteristic denial; an inability to perceive others' reactions; regressive, dependent unconscious group-as-a-whole forces; his ineffective interpretation of his organizational role; or a combination of all four factors.

Assessment thus served two major purposes in this case. The first was to elevate the importance of increased self-awareness as an objective for the coaching process. The second was to help formulate another set of hypotheses—and a concomitant set of questions—about what was eliciting the client's behaviors. In essence, assessment had confirmed the need for more assessment—and it would continue to figure prominently throughout the process.

ANNOTATED BIBLIOGRAPHY

Argyris, C. (1952). Diagnosing defenses against the outsider. *Journal of Social Issues, 8,* 24–34.
Enumerates the common forms of individual and institutional resistance organizational consultants encounter when attempting to conduct interviews.

Kahn, R. L., & Cannell, C. F. (1965). Motivating respondents, setting objectives, designing questions, and probing to meet objectives. In *The dynamics of interviewing* (pp. 106–232). New York: Wiley.
Comprehensive guidelines for the design and construction of effective interview protocols.

Kaplan, A. (1964). The process of observation in behavioral science. In *The conduct of inquiry* (pp. 126–144). San Francisco, CA: Chandler.
A remarkable section in a remarkable book about scientific method in the behavioral sciences.

Kernberg, O. M. (1998). Leadership and organizational functioning; Regression in organizational leadership. In *Ideology, conflict, and leadership in groups and organizations* (pp. 51–90). New Haven, CT: Yale University Press.
An exposition of the impact of systemic forces on individual leaders in organizations.

Shea, S. C. (1988). *Psychiatric interviewing: The art of understanding.* Philadelphia, PA: W. B. Saunders.
Comprehensive treatise on diagnostic interviewing skills.

Sullivan, H. S. (1970). *The psychiatric interview.* New York: W.W. Norton.
This is the classic by a master diagnostic interviewer. It contains discussions not only on interviewing technique but also on participant-observation, analysis of interactional patterns, and exploring resistance.

Whyte, W. F. & Whyte, K. K. (1984). *Learning from the field: A guide from experience.* Beverly Hills, CA: Sage.
Chapter 6 is an essential reading to gain an understanding of the interviewing techniques, particularly the unstructured interview, utilized in the assessment phase of Multidimensional Coaching.

In addition, because Jeanne was as hard on others as she was on herself, she created an environment in which others were afraid to make a mistake.

I paused to make certain Jeanne was absorbing the information. She indicated that none of it surprised her, so I went on. I told her that I believed at the heart of most of her problems was her need to either have everything done perfectly by everyone around her, or to do it herself so that it would be perfect. I explained that this set up a vicious cycle in which her direct reports did not learn and were not accountable, thereby impeding her ability to either develop her staff or to replace those who were truly incapable of doing the work. This created a situation in which she, herself, was required to do all the work, resulting in her feeling overwhelmed and angry, which, in turn, caused her to be abrupt and reactive with those around her. They, then, became fearful of making a mistake and unwilling to take on new challenges, thus perpetuating the cycle. We talked about the fact that the only way out of this was for her to allow her direct reports to do the work, including allowing mistakes to occur. The nature and frequency of the mistakes would determine whether people were learning or whether they had to be replaced. We also talked about the fact that delegation did not mean abrogation of responsibility to oversee the effort. In light of previous discussions about relinquishing the need to universally produce A+ work, she said that she was ready to delegate and step back.

I concluded the feedback report with other areas that been mentioned, but which we had already discussed in earlier meetings: the need to listen, seek input, and not interrupt; the need to modify the quickness with which certain decisions were made and imposed; the need to have others understand the importance of their work by including the bigger picture; the immediate cessation of public reprimands; and limiting of the use of e-mail, replacing it with more face-to-face communication.

Jeanne expressed relief when the feedback ended. She said that nothing had been a surprise and that we had already discussed most of the significant areas. She was gratified by what had been described as strengths and determined to improve in the areas that were impeding her effectiveness and the growth and development of her staff. I asked her to think about the feedback until our next meeting and invited her to call me if she had any questions or needed to discuss anything before then.

THE CASE OF JACK (continued)

Jack appeared nervous at the feedback session. He was uncharacteristically serious and brought a pad and pen to the conference table. I told him that it was not necessary to take notes, as I would be giving him a written report. I began by reporting on what I saw as the context in which he was working—a government agency with a clear hierarchy but not always very clear lines of authority. In addition, the complexity of the task of his unit, combined with the high visibility of the work and extremely demanding clients, made his job particularly difficult. As a result, the role expectations placed on him were equally demanding and complex: leadership that provided vision, inspiration, and direction to others; high-level decision making, which empowered others to make lower-level decisions; highly visible "public relations" for the unit; and liaison to senior management. His list of strengths was long and centered on his technical skills, his attention to details, his commitment to the organization, and a universal belief in his human decency. There were three clear areas for improvement: delegation, motivation, and leadership. He was perceived as a micromanager who used intimidation to move others, focusing on their weaknesses rather than their strengths, and who did not display a sense of vision or an ability to build a cohesive team.

Throughout the feedback, Jack was extremely attentive. He was visibly uncomfortable listening to the strengths. He was serious and focused when listening to the weaknesses. When I concluded the report, he looked at me and remarked, "You have a lot of hard work with me." When I reminded him of what had been reported about his strengths, he said all of the credit for those went to his parents and his brother. He then referred to a specific area that had been mentioned regarding leadership—his inability to confront others. He explained that he had only seen his father cry once. It had happened after a disagreement between his father and his mother. Jack attributed his difficulty to confront others to this and stated that he believed this was also the source of difficulties in his marriage. I asked him what he thought would happen if he addressed difficult issues at work. "I don't know," he responded quietly. We agreed that that was an area we should work on.

"I remember leadership and motivation. What was the third area you mentioned?" Jack next asked. "Delegation," I responded. "Oh, that's right. They think I'm a micromanager. Are you sure? I don't think I micromanage." I suggested we might want to look at the discrepancy in perceptions over the course of our work.

THE CASE OF CARA

Because the perceptions of Cara's areas for improvement were significant, I spent a considerable amount of time explaining the concept of context and embedded behavior. In previous sessions, she had shown an interest in theory,

ANALYSIS: THE CASES OF KEN AND SONIA

In the first case, it was the contrast in the client's behavior that generated the working hypotheses. Had objectives setting remained within the confines of the first meeting, it would have been difficult to understand why lack of leadership had emerged so prominently in the feedback. With the consultant, the client took full ownership for formulating incisive and compelling objectives with strongly positive implications for himself and his department. A very different set of behaviors, however, surfaced during the three-way meeting. Here, the client appeared to be entirely invested in maintaining a subservient, and very junior, role. The question, of course, was why he was engaged in this collusion. Several hypotheses were formulated: (1) It was most important to him to have the support of his manager, so he would adopt any behavior that was necessary to maintain it. (2) Unconscious forces in the group required that someone take on this role, and Ken, because of his age, was unconsciously complying. (3) This was the relationship he had had with his father, and he was unconsciously repeating it in the work environment. (4) Because his manager was old enough to be his father, this was a sign of respect. (5) Maintaining the posture of the inexperienced, young manager who needed the help and support of all those around him was a way to avoid dealing with some of the more unpleasant aspects of his job. The nature of the work with this client would be greatly influenced by which hypotheses were supported by further data as the coaching process continued.

In the second case, it was not the client's behavior, but rather the manager's that sparked a new set of hypotheses. In this case, the efficiency of objectives setting in the first meeting had been predictable. In characteristic fashion, the client had seized the opportunity to take full responsibility for reviewing the existing information and translating it into actionable language against which she could execute. Also as expected, in the second meeting the client's professionalism and warmth were palpable. Her behavior not only supported the hypothesis that her interpersonal skills were proficient with authority figures but made clear that the emotional connection she had formed was completely authentic. Given the relationship between the two women and the manager's repeated declarations of support, it was surprising that the latter was willing to dismiss the data that had been the very reason that coaching had been initiated and in doing so, was, however unconsciously, undermining the client's efforts. The client's respectful challenge demonstrated that she would not collude with the denial and was committed to change.

As a result of the objectives-setting meetings, the consultant formulated three interrelated hypotheses. The first was that, for the manager to behave in so dichotomous a fashion, there were in operation powerful unconscious organizational forces to prevent the client from changing. The second was that there would be a concomitant pull on the consultant, as a result of repeated organizational entry and the already obvious similarities in interaction between the consultant and the client and the manager and the client, to dismiss the importance of the client's objectives. The third was that the client, faced with these influences, would approach coaching in the same way as she approached all of her objectives—as simply another of the many tasks that she was so adept at executing with resolute determination and uncompromising perfection. The ability of the consultant to remain vigilant to these forces and, in turn, help the client become aware of them, would prove critical in the work ahead.

ANNOTATED BIBLIOGRAPHY

Kanfer, F. H., & Gaelick-Buys, L. (1991). In F. H. Kanfer & A. P. Goldstein (Eds.), *Helping people change: A textbook of methods* (4th ed., pp.305–360). New York: Pergamon Press.
   An excellent discussion of the rationale for and the components of behavioral self-management, including the need to articulate clear objectives.

CHAPTER 11

Formal Coaching

As the preceding chapters have continually espoused, executive coaching must be viewed as a process that focuses on more than the individual and more than what is conscious. It regards the organization and its components as active participants rather than as a contextual backdrop and therefore treats every individual intervention as a simultaneous organizational intervention. It explores every observable action for underlying meaning and examines behavior in light of a multitude of forces—not only intrapsychic and organizational but also interpersonal, group, and intergroup—and maintains that those forces have unconscious elements that are, at minimum, as powerful as to those that are conscious. It affirms that the consultant, upon entering the organization, is subject to the same forces and therefore requires that the consultant engage in self-reflection and self-scrutiny in order to use himself/herself as a finely calibrated instrument with which to formulate and test hypotheses, to monitor individual and organizational change, and to select and implement appropriate interventions, which can be as varied as the objectives of the client and the forces that influence the client's behaviors.

It is during this, the formal coaching stage, that the interventions become most apparent. The consultant, with the utmost respect for individual and organizational readiness, regularly meets with the client, continuously assesses what the client needs, and chooses from among an extensive repertoire of methods and techniques the most appropriate intervention at any given point in the work with the client.

There are, therefore, three essential requirements for effectiveness during formal coaching. The first is the comprehensive understanding of the client and the organization acquired from all that has preceded this phase. The second is a planned and purposeful venue in which the formal coaching can occur. The third is a thorough knowledge of the widest possible array of coaching techniques and methods. Each of these is discussed in detail below.

THE FOUNDATION: PRECEDING STAGES

Figure 11.1 is a vivid depiction of coaching as the pinnacle of a much larger process in which each previous stage contributes to the efficacy of the next.

It is only with clearly articulated objectives that it is possible to formulate a meaningful coaching plan, to measure progress and ultimate success, and to invite into the process relevant others whose acceptance and reinforcement of change is crucial. It is only with thorough, reliable, and relevant feedback, and the client's openness to receive it, that it is possible to determine the most critical objectives. It is only with comprehensive assessment, and the methodology to conduct it, that it is possible to prepare, analyze, and deliver thorough feedback. It is only with willing participation by the organization and the client that it is possible to conduct assessment. It is only with the establishment of a solid working alliance between the client and the consultant that it is possible for engagement in the coaching process to occur. It is only with a robust and cogent theory to guide and inform every phase of coaching that it is possible to have a sound executive coaching process. And it is only with a sound process that it is possible to foster the fundamental goals of coaching—expanded self-awareness and sustained change.

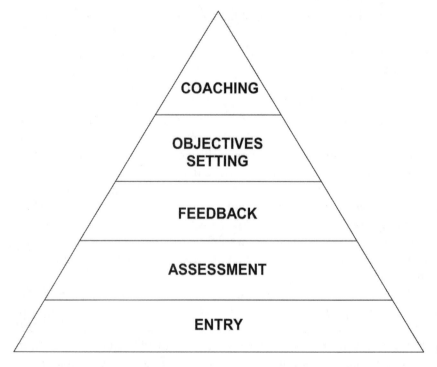

FIGURE 11.1 Coaching and preceding phases.

THE VENUE: REGULARLY SCHEDULED MEETINGS

Regularly scheduled meetings form the basis of a reiterative and recursive cycle of consistent progression toward coaching objectives. Although the focus in each meeting can be quite different, certain core elements are constant across meetings and clients. These elements include the deepening alliance between the consultant and the client, and assignments that will bring the client closer to attaining his/her goals. As represented in Figure 11.2, there are six recurrent components:

1. Reconnect: The client and the consultant take the time to reestablish their connection in whatever way is most comfortable for the client.
2. Update: The client briefs the consultant on what has occurred at work since the last meeting.
3. Review homework: The client shares his/her experiences with the assignment, which usually consists of some form of behavioral experimentation and some provision for self-observation and reflection. Together, the client and the consultant identify and explore the relative ease or difficulty in completing the assignment and the client's observations about himself/herself in attempting to complete it.
4. Analyze factors: The client and the consultant identify the individual and contextual factors that led to the ease or difficulty of completing the assignment to determine how these factors can be either reinforced or mitigated in the future.
5. Assign new homework: After positively reinforcing the client for progress made thus far, the consultant assigns a new action that is progressively more challenging than the last.
6. Schedule next meeting: The client and the consultant agree on the date and time of the next meeting, taking into consideration the length of time required to adequately complete the new assignment.

In a perfect world, the progression would be linear, with each meeting building on the previous one and change occurring incrementally. Executives, however, do not live in a perfect world. Organizational exigencies are a part of daily life, and the consultant, as a trusted advisor, must be prepared to work with the client on emerging issues as they arise (see Figure 11.3).

Other issues, linked not to conscious organizational priorities but to unconscious reactions to the coaching process, may also arise. As assignments become more difficult for the client, or as change in the client becomes more apparent to the organization, resistance may become inevitable. The client might find reasons not to do assignments or encounter powerful obstacles while

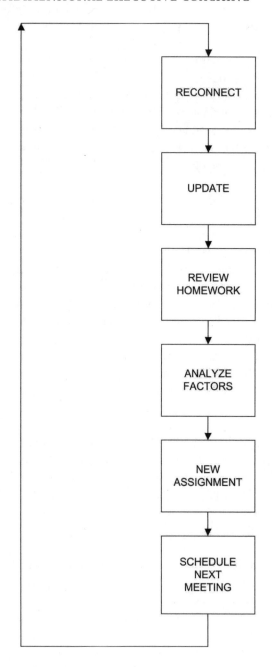

FIGURE 11.2 Basic components of coaching meetings.

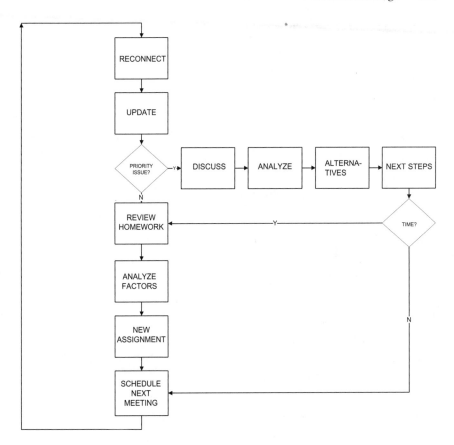

FIGURE 11.3 Coaching meetings—unexpected priorities.

attempting to complete assignments. It is at this juncture that exploration of resistance, whether intrapsychic or organizational, becomes essential, and the client's insight becomes the pathway to further progress (see Figure 11.4).

As is immediately apparent, there are three paths in the coaching cycle. The middle path of the chart generally occurs during the very early part of coaching, when easier behavioral practice is assigned, and during the final stage of coaching, when the objectives have been achieved and are being reinforced. If all meetings follow this path, however, the consultant must consider whether the assignments should be more challenging, the objectives should be revised, or the client does not need the help of a coach in achieving them. The path on the right can occur during any point in

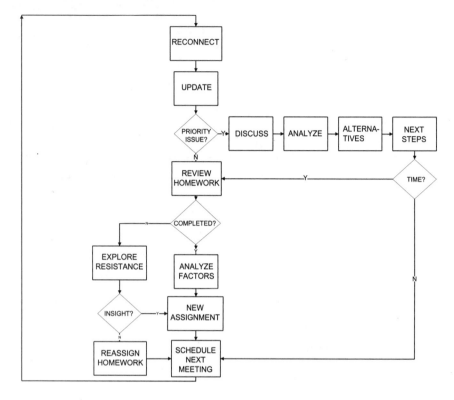

FIGURE 11.4 Coaching meetings—full cycle.

coaching. In the most ideal of circumstances, these emerging issues and the manner in which they might be addressed can readily be linked to the coaching objectives and used for deeper learning; if however, every meeting follows this path and continuously diverts attention from the attainment of stated coaching objectives, the consultant must question whether this is a form of resistance and intervene accordingly. The path on the left of the chart illustrates what occurs when seemingly insurmountable obstacles arise. The consultant and the client together explore the nature and source of the impediment and whether it is a form of unconscious resistance in the client, the context, or both. If so, based entirely on what appears to be the client's readiness to acknowledge the resistance, the consultant determines the relative gentleness or forcefulness of the intervention. Sometimes, a flash of insight proves pivotal to the remainder of the coaching process; sometimes the insight emerges more slowly. Consequently, there are intervals in the cycle in which progress can be made without

CHAPTER 12

Outcome Evaluation[1]

Consultants who have worked with executives, or have themselves held executive positions, can readily attest to the fact that these senior managers and their organizational sponsors want to know that their endeavors have been successful. This is no less true of their efforts in the coaching process than of any other facet of their business lives. Outcome evaluation, then, is a vital aspect of the coaching process.

Consultants who have made, or wish to make, significant contributions to the field can readily attest to the fact that if executive coaching is ever to take up its place as a recognized profession, it will need to be supported by a substantive body of empirical research that encompasses the scientific substantiation of coaching efficacy. While developing accepted evaluation methodologies is receiving greater attention, there are few studies that provide the basis for deeper empirical investigation. Outcome evaluation, then, is a vital avenue for further research.

One of the most powerful differentiators of the approach presented in this book is that it concerns itself with measuring efficacy and outcomes. It does so not only by integrating evaluation into the coaching process from its inception, but also by providing a framework for statistically sound measures capable of contributing to the empirical base of research.

METHOD 1: OBJECTIVES

As discussed in Chapter 10, objectives and objectives setting are an inherent part of the coaching process. If articulated well, they provide the basis on

[1] An earlier version of the material in this chapter appears in Orenstein, R. L. (2006). Measuring executive coaching efficacy? The answer was right here all the time. *Consulting Psychology Journal: Practice and Research, 58*(2), 106–116. Copyright 2006 by the American Psychological Association. All sections and tables taken from that article are adapted or reprinted with permission.

which all those involved in coaching have a vehicle with which to measure progress and ultimate success. The ease, simplicity, and familiarity of objectives as a measure of performance make evaluation accessible at any point in the coaching process, and, as such, the method is readily embraced by coaching clients. When objectives become the measure of choice, the outcome evaluation occurs within the planned scope of the coaching contract in the form of the final meeting among the client, the client's manager, and the consultant (see Chapter 13). If these individuals agree that the objectives have been achieved, the coaching assignment is considered successful, and the coaching work is considered concluded.

Clearly, this is the most subjective of the methods and the one least likely to be considered a science. It is, however, the method most frequently used in practice, primarily owing to its ease of use and resemblance to other organizational performance measures.

METHOD 2: INTERVIEWS

It is sometimes the case that a client, or the client's manager, wishes to have wider validation of coaching outcomes and requests that the 360-degree process be repeated in whole or part. Themes that emerge from the second series of interviews can be compared to the original in order to examine degrees of change, and emerging themes can be examined to determine if additional developmental work is needed. If the coaching engagement has spanned a 9- to 12-month period, a long enough time frame for perceptions to have changed for those not actively involved in the process, the contract can be extended, and the interviews can be conducted before the conclusion of the coaching engagement. If the span of time from the previous interviews is less than 9 months, the interviews take place after the coaching assignment has concluded, and a new contract is created.

Repeating the interview process undeniably increases the reliability of outcome evaluation. Additionally, if interviewees who were not part of the original process are added and the interviewer is someone other than the consultant who provided the coaching, reliability is further ensured by mitigating bias from those with a direct investment in positive outcomes. This method, while attractive in terms of its strength in corroborating outcomes, is selected less frequently by clients because of the additional time and costs involved.

METHOD 3: THE EMPATHIC ORGANIC QUESTIONNAIRE

When a client wishes to have statistically sound evidence of coaching outcomes and efficacy, there currently exists no tool more relevant than the Empathic Organic Questionnaire (Alderfer & Brown, 1972; Orenstein, 2006).

Encompassing the most rigorous of both qualitative and quantitative research methodologies, it is an instrument whose content is derived from qualitative interviews but which lends itself to quantitative statistical analysis through a five-stage process:

1. Designing the instrument.
2. Selecting the respondents.
3. Administering the questionnaire.
4. Analyzing the data.
5. Evaluating results.

Designing the Instrument

There are seven steps in designing the questionnaire:

1. Based on a review of the client's feedback report, coaching objectives, and coaching focus, broad areas for examination are selected.
2. Exact quotes and phrases pertinent to the identified areas are extracted from the qualitative interviews conducted at the start of the executive coaching process.
3. The quotes and phrases are converted into questionnaire items by expressing a single thought for each, presenting each thought positively and negatively to eliminate bias (Miller & Fagley, 1991), and selecting an equal number of items for each area.
4. To enhance statistical soundness, additional methods for arriving at the data are then added (Campbell & Fiske, 1959): To strengthen reliability and convergent validity, an open-ended question is included; to ensure discriminant validity and to counteract the demand characteristic caused by retrospective ratings, a control category consisting of items for which change was neither desired nor sought is added.
5. To further eliminate bias, the order of all items is randomly mixed.
6. The items are converted to past tense and again randomly reordered.
7. The final instrument is organized into past- and present-tense versions (see Appendix E).

Selecting the Respondents

The respondents are selected so as to constitute a representative sample of the universe of relevant others. The sample should be large enough to ensure adequate degrees of freedom for later statistical calculations[2] and to include relevant others who are unbiased by previous participation, while also being an acceptable number for the organization. Respondents are selected by the client, in consultation with the consultant, and should include the original interviewees and additional individuals selected for diversity in age, gender, race, ethnicity, and hierarchical level, so as to represent the demographics of the client's organization.

Administering the Questionnaire

The client contacts the respondents to request participation in the evaluation process and to notify them that a consultant will be calling. In order to avoid bias, the questionnaire is administered by a consultant whom the respondents have not previously met. In order to assure completion, the consultant calls each respondent to arrange an individual appointment, asking that the respondent secure a private room in order to complete the questionnaire. At the scheduled time, the consultant reviews the procedure with the respondent, including both the voluntary nature of participation and the manner in which confidentiality will be safeguarded, gives each respondent the instrument and an unmarked envelope in which to seal it, and waits outside the room until the respondent emerges with the completed questionnaire in the sealed envelope.

Analyzing the Data

When all the questionnaires are collected, the open-ended data in each document is reviewed and compared to the numerical responses for validation purposes (i.e., to make certain that positive responses match positive statements, and vice versa). All open-ended data are then copied verbatim to a separate document. Next, each of the past-tense items is matched to the corresponding present-tense item. Negatively worded items are reverse scored in order to achieve numerical consistency for analytical purposes. A paired samples t-test at an alpha level of .05 is performed on all items.

Evaluating Results

The results of the t-tests are examined in three categories. The first category is composed of those items directly related to the coaching objectives; the second category consists of those items indirectly related to the coaching

---

[2] For a complete discussion of degrees of freedom, reliability, and confidence intervals, readers are directed to Keppel, G., Saufley, W. H., Jr., & Tokunaga, H. (1983). *Introduction to design and analysis: A student's handbook* (2nd ed.). New York: W. H. Freeman; and Cohen & Cohen (1983). *Applied Multiple Regression/Correlation Analysis for the Behavioral Sciences* (2nd ed.). New Jersey: Lawrence Erlbaum.

objectives; and the third category comprises the control items, considered unrelated to the coaching objectives. A predominance of significant items in the first category, fewer significant items in the second category, and none in the third indicate that coaching outcomes have been achieved.

For those seriously interested in the soundness of outcome evaluation, the benefits of using the empathic organic questionnaire are obvious. Nonetheless, there are factors that must be carefully considered. First and foremost, the methodology is entirely reliant on a comprehensive process that supports it. Therefore, none of the preceding interrelated elements of multidimensional coaching can be eliminated, particularly the following: conducting in-depth qualitative interviews with relevant participants that ultimately provide the content for the organic instrument, involve the respondents in the client's process of change, and enable the development of relationships that will increase the likelihood of willing participation in postcoaching assessment; intensive feedback aggregated from the interview data that will provide the broad areas for later evaluation; and the formulation of specific coaching objectives and outcome criteria that are the basis of the statistical analysis.

Second, the method requires more of the consultant than effective practice skills. An understanding of research design and statistical analysis is essential. Equally significant is the obligation to take an investigative and reflective stance in relation to one's own work, and thereby to be willing to accept, with brutal honesty, when that work has not been effective and when it must be refined, transformed, or even abandoned in favor of more efficacious approaches.

The third factor involves the rigors of instrument design and administration. The content for the organic questionnaire, by its very nature and what it seeks to measure, cannot be standardized, even when individuals being coached are part of the same client system. It must be constructed on a case-by-case basis, each time following the requirements for statistical validity. In addition, to ensure reliability, it must be administered in such a way as to maximize willing participation from selected respondents who constitute a representative sample of the universe of relevant others. It is thus a time-consuming and labor-intensive tool, and all those involved must believe in the worthiness of the evaluation effort.

The case that concludes this chapter demonstrates a situation in which those involved were convinced of the value of the Empathic Organic Questionnaire and committed to engage in the process.

THE CASE OF HENRY

The request to work with Henry, a senior executive in a large state agency, came from his immediate manager. The latter explained that the client had flagrantly dismissed the results of a recently conducted 360-degree assessment that had indicated, in addition to weakness in the areas of communication, interpersonal relations, and motivation, that Henry's self-evaluation in all areas was considerably higher than those of his peers, subordinates, and manager. The manager also described the client as arrogant, domineering, and defensive.

When I met with Henry, he was cold and aloof. He stated that the assessment had been of no value to him because, while the results of the standardized instrument indicated what people thought, it explained neither why they arrived at their conclusions nor how he could improve. Furthermore, his manager had chosen the respondents and would not identify them, so Henry was precluded from speaking with them to discover the answers to his questions. He had concluded that the results were meaningless because he assumed they had been skewed by one individual on his staff with whom he had had significant problems for many years. Interactions with his manager had become strained over the course of the previous year, so communication had been limited between them, and their meeting to discuss the results had worsened their relationship. He was unwilling to undergo any similar assessment process.

When I described the process that I used, Henry became more responsive. He quickly recognized how the approach differed from the experience he had recently undergone. He decided, albeit still with some skepticism, to engage in executive coaching. He selected 15 people, including senior managers, peers, subordinates, and customers, with whom the interviews were to be conducted, and the assessment phase began.

The feedback that I shared with Henry after the interview data had been aggregated and analyzed was revelatory to him. He was disappointed (and more than a little surprised) that it corroborated some of the standardized data and that it could not be attributed to a single disgruntled employee, but he was relieved that he could ask questions and learn the underlying reasons for the findings. In addition, he was gratified to learn of the strengths that had been identified and that they could be leveraged during the coaching phase. He also seemed fascinated by the explanation of organizational and group forces that had surfaced over the course of the interviews. The coaching objectives he formulated fell within the originally identified areas of motivation, communication, and interpersonal skills but were much more specific: To increase recognition of staff; to become more approachable, caring and patient; and to eliminate public criticism, fear, and intimidation.

During the intensive coaching that followed, Henry remained highly motivated. An initial reluctance to divulge any personal information to me disappeared after the feedback session, and we were able to discuss how systemic forces were triggering unconscious and self-defeating patterns. Our interactions, which had previously caused me to question whether a successful working alliance could be established, now evoked compassion and empathy. This mirrored the positive responses he was receiving from his staff, including many of those who had been involved in the interview process. They reinforced his efforts, and he was excited and pleased. At the end of 6 months, Henry felt confident that he had achieved the stated coaching objectives, and we met with his manager for his confirmation. The latter agreed that he had seen dramatic differences in Henry's behavior and expressed a desire to conduct another 360-degree assessment that would provide some quantitative indication of outcomes. When I described the organic questionnaire and suggested using it in place of the standardized instrument, both Henry and the manager readily agreed. We decided to wait another 6 months before conducting the evaluation in order to make certain that the behavior changes, and perceptions about them, were permanent.

When it was time to construct the questionnaire, I reviewed Henry's feedback report, his coaching objectives, and our focus throughout coaching. The data indicated that emphasis should be placed on outcomes in the areas of motivation, communication, and interpersonal skills. Direct quotes and phrases relevant to the identified areas were extracted from the 15 qualitative interviews conducted at the start of the executive coaching process. The control category consisted of the items considered strengths, which we had not sought to change in any way during the coaching process (see Figure 12.1 for the final version of the instrument).

Before beginning the evaluation, Henry and I identified 20 respondents— the original 15 and 5 additional individuals selected for appropriate diversity. This resulted in a respondent group representative of the demographics of his organization: 12 males (10 Whites, 1 African-American, 1 Hispanic) ranging in age from 26 to 63 and 8 females (3 Whites, 2 African-Americans, and 2 Hispanics) ranging in age from 32 to 52, representing levels from first-line supervisor through vice president.

Henry called the respondents to request participation in the evaluation process and to notify them that a consultant would be calling. The questionnaire was administered by my business partner, whom the respondents had not previously met.

Tables 12.1 through 12.4 show the results of the analysis.

In the first category, those items directly related to coaching objectives, 15 of the 19 items were significant, 6 at an alpha level of .05, 6 at an alpha level of .01, and 3 at an alpha level of .001. In the second category, items indirectly related, 4 of the 11 items were significant, 2 at an alpha level of .05 and 2 at an alpha level of .01. In the third category, the control, none of the items were significant. Both Henry and I were thrilled with the results; his manager was fully satisfied that Henry had achieved his objectives; and the coaching, in this case, was considered a proven success.

Figure 12.1*

EXECUTIVE COACHING EVALUATION

Dear Evaluator:

The purpose of this evaluation is to discover the effects, if any, of executive coaching on the behaviors of those who undergo the process. Therefore, your perceptions in the present and the past are crucial.

This evaluation has four sections:

- Section I asks you to reflect on your interactions with XXXX approximately 9–12 months ago and to describe his professional behavior at that time.

- Section II contains a series of statements about *past* behaviors. Please indicate the extent to which you agree or disagree with each in relation to XXXX.

- Section III asks you to reflect on your interactions with XXXX currently and to describe his professional behavior at the present time.

- Section IV contains the same statements about *present* behaviors. Again, please indicate the extent to which you agree or disagree with each in relation to XXXX.

All of your responses will be treated with complete confidentially.

Thank you very much for providing this information.

---

* From "Measuring Executive Coaching Efficacy" by R.L. Orenstein, *Consulting Psychology Journal*, 58 (2), p. 111. Copyright 2006 by the American Psychological Association. Reprinted with permission.

Section I

Directions: Please reflect on your interactions with XXXX approximately *9 to 12 months ago*. In the space below, briefly describe what XXXX was like as a professional. Then, please answer the questions in the following sections.

Section II

Directions: Please indicate to what extent you agree or disagree with the following statements about XXXX as they describe his behavior approximately 9–12 months ago. Please place a check mark in the appropriate box.

Key: 1. Disagree completely
2. Disagree somewhat
3. Neither agree nor disagree
4. Agree somewhat
5. Agree completely

	1	2	3	4	5
1. He backed me up when I made a mistake.					
2. He behaved in unpredictable ways.					
3. He belittled me.					
4. He cared about me.					
5. I found him personable and approachable.					
6. I noticed that his moods changed quickly.					
7. He demonstrated strong organizational skills.					
8. He did not value my opinion.					
9. He got the job done.					
10. He gave me credit when I did a good job.					
11. I considered him a visionary.					
12. I considered him a bully.					
13. He gave the right job to the right person.					
14. He hindered me from growing professionally.					
15. He interrupted me when I spoke.					
16. He was fair to me.					
17. He helped me be the best I could be.					
18. I saw him criticize others in public.					

Key: 1. Disagree completely
2. Disagree somewhat
3. Neither agree nor disagree
4. Agree somewhat
5. Agree completely

	1	2	3	4	5
19. He was impatient with me					
20. He was cold to me.					
21. He was not interested in details.					
22. I didn't know how to read him.					
23. I enjoyed his sense of humor.					
24. He was not there when I needed him.					
25. He was not visible to customers.					
26. He was straightforward and clear in our communications.					
27. He isolated himself from his staff.					
28. He listened when I spoke to him.					
29. He talked above my level.					
30. He welcomed it when I challenged him.					
31. I was afraid to be honest with him.					
32. I considered him opinionated.					
33. He did not hold a grudge.					
34. I found him easy to get along with.					
35. I observed him leading by example.					
36. He intimidated me.					
37. I saw him get upset quickly.					
38. I trusted him.					
39. When I met with him, I was on guard.					
40. He set high standards of performance.					

Section III

Directions: Please reflect on your interactions with XXXX currently. In the space below, briefly describe what XXXX is like as a professional. Then, please answer the questions in the following sections.

Section IV

Directions: Please indicate to what extent you agree or disagree with the following statements about XXXX as they describe his behavior currently. Please place a check mark in the appropriate box.

Key: 1. Disagree completely
2. Disagree somewhat
3. Neither agree nor disagree
4. Agree somewhat
5. Agree completely

	1	2	3	4	5
1. He gives the right job to the right person.					
2. I find him personable and approachable.					
3. He is not interested in details.					
4. He is fair to me.					
5. He isolates himself from his staff.					
6. He listens when I speak to him.					
7. He is not there when I need him.					
8. I observe him leading by example.					
9. I find him easy to get along with.					
10. He helps me be the best I can be.					
11. He hinders me from growing professionally.					
12. He behaves in unpredictable ways.					
13. When I meet with him, I am on guard.					
14. He gives me credit when I do a good job.					
15. I am afraid to be honest with him.					
16. I see him criticize others in public.					
17. I trust him.					
18. I consider him opinionated.					
19. I notice that his moods change quickly.					

Key: 1. Disagree completely
2. Disagree somewhat
3. Neither agree nor disagree
4. Agree somewhat
5. Agree completely

	1	2	3	4	5
20. He is impatient with me.					
21. I don't know how to read him.					
22. I enjoy his sense of humor.					
23. He cares about me.					
24. I consider him a visionary.					
25. I consider him a bully.					
26. He demonstrates strong organizational skills.					
27. He interrupts me when I speak.					
28. He does not value my opinion.					
29. He backs me up when I make a mistake.					
30. He welcomes it when I challenge him.					
31. He intimidates me.					
32. He sets high standards of performance.					
33. He belittles me.					
34. He is straightforward and clear in our communications.					
35. I see him get upset quickly.					
36. He is not visible to customers.					
37. He is cold to me.					
38. He does not hold a grudge.					
39. He talks above my level.					
40. He gets the job done.					

TABLE 12.1.   Behaviors Directly Related to Coaching Objectives

Item	Mean past	Mean present	N	P
He belittles me. (R)	3.8	4.1	18	.38
He cares about me.	2.7	3.6	18	.01**
I find him personable and approachable.	2.8	4.1	20	.00**
He does not value my opinion. (R)	3.4	3.7	19	.43
He gives me credit when I do a good job.	3.7	4.2	18	.01*
I consider him a bully. (R)	2.9	3.8	18	.00**
He interrupts me when I speak. (R)	2.7	3.5	19	.00***
He helps me be the best I can be.	3.2	3.8	19	.02*
I see him criticize others in public. (R)	2.6	4.2	17	.00***
He is impatient with me. (R)	2.3	3.6	19	.00***
He is cold to me. (R)	3.2	4.6	20	.01**
I don't know how to read him. (R)	2.7	3.7	19	.00**
He is not there when I need him. (R)	3.8	4.3	19	.04*
He isolates himself from his staff. (R)	3.5	4.4	19	.03*
He listens when I speak to him.	3.7	4.2	20	.04*
He welcomes it when I challenge him.	2.8	3.2	18	.05*
I am afraid to be honest with him. (R)	3.8	4.3	20	.07
He intimidates me. (R)	3.4	3.8	20	.23
When I meet with him, I am on guard. (R)	2.9	3.9	19	.00**

Source: From "Measuring Executive Coaching Efficacy" by R. L. Orenstein, *Consulting Psychology Journal, 58*(2), p. 111. Copyright 2006 by the American Psychological Association. Reprinted with permission.

(R) indicates reverse scored item.

p < .05. **p* < .01. ***p* < .001.

TABLE 12.2.   Behaviors Indirectly Related to Coaching Objectives

Item	Mean past	Mean present	N	p
He behaves in unpredictable ways. (R)	3.1	3.5	18	.36
I notice that his moods change quickly. (R)	2.6	3.4	18	.08
He is fair to me.	3.8	4.1	20	.08
He is not interested in details. (R)	2.1	2.6	19	.04*
He is not visible to customers. (R)	3.4	4.2	19	.01*
He talks above my level. (R)	4.1	4.3	19	.27
I consider him opinionated. (R)	1.8	2.1	18	.24

(Continued)

TABLE 12.2. *(Continued)*

Item	Mean past	Mean present	N	p
He does not hold a grudge.	3.4	3.7	19	.40
I find him easy to get along with.	3.3	3.6	20	.27
I observe him leading by example.	3.6	4.2	18	.00**
I see him get upset quickly. (R)	2.2	3.7	18	.00**

Source: From "Measuring Executive Coaching Efficacy" by R. L. Orenstein, *Consulting Psychology Journal, 58*(2), p. 111. Copyright 2006 by the American Psychological Association. Reprinted with permission.

(R) indicates reverse scored item.

p < .05. **p* < .01.

TABLE 12.3.   Strengths (Control Category)

Item	Mean past	Mean present	N	p
He backs me up when I make a mistake.	3.6	3.8	18	.24
He demonstrates strong organizational skills.	4.8	4.8	20	1.00
He gets the job done.	4.6	4.6	19	1.00
I consider him a visionary.	3.9	4.2	17	.08
He gives the right job to the right person.	3.9	4.2	18	.22
He hinders me from growing professionally. (R)	3.8	4.2	18	.11
I enjoy his sense of humor.	3.7	3.8	18	.50
He is straightforward and clear in our communications.	4.1	4.4	20	.08
I trust him.	3.7	3.9	20	.23
He sets high standards of performance.	4.6	4.5	19	.58

Source: From "Measuring Executive Coaching Efficacy" by R. L. Orenstein, *Consulting Psychology Journal, 58*(2), p. 111. Copyright 2006 by the American Psychological Association. Reprinted with permission.

(R) indicates reverse scored item.

TABLE 12.4.   Mean Differences by Category

Category	Mean past	Mean present	Mean difference
Directly related	3.1	4.0	0.9
Indirectly related	3.0	3.6	0.6
Control	4.1	4.2	0.1

Source: From "Measuring Executive Coaching Efficacy" by R. L.Orenstein, *Consulting Psychology Journal, 58*(2), p. 111. Copyright 2006 by the American Psychological Association. Reprinted with permission.

ANNOTATED BIBLIOGRAPHY

Alderfer, C. P. & Brown, L. D. (1972). Designing an "empathic questionnaire" for organizational research. *Journal of Applied Psychology, 56*, 456–460.
The original work and well worth reading.
Campbell, D. T. & Fiske, D. W. (1959). Convergent & discriminant validation by the multi-trait multi-method matrix. *Psychological Bulletin, 56*, 81–105.
Required reading for those using qualitative methodology who are also interested in statistical reliability and validity.
Isaac, S. & Michael, W. B. (1995). *Handbook in research and evaluation: A collection of principles, methods, and strategies useful in the planning, design, and evaluation of studies in education and the behavioral sciences* (3rd ed.). San Diego, CA: EdITS.
A review of the fundamentals of research design and methodology, intentionally written for clarity and brevity.

CHAPTER 13

Concluding the Coaching Process

There are three ways in which coaching can end: (1) as a planned and essential step in the process of achieving objectives, (2) as a result of the expiration of the contract, or (3) through unexpected early termination. Each of these outcomes has important implications and must be handled with the same sensitivity and thoughtfulness as any other aspect of the work.

The happiest of reasons for ending coaching is, of course, attainment of coaching objectives. When it becomes apparent that the client is close to achieving objectives, preparation for ending the work begins. The consultant recommends that longer periods of time elapse between scheduled meetings, thereby allowing the client to self-manage, while still providing positive reinforcement. If the client maintains the behavior change for several months, the consultant suggests that it is time to conclude coaching. If the client agrees, the evaluation meeting with the client's manager is held. Together, the client, the client's manager, and the consultant discuss observable outcomes, the need for continuous reinforcement by the manager, and further developmental opportunities. Subsequently, in the final meeting between the client and the consultant, the most significant learnings are reviewed and documented, and the consultant suggests that the client review them on a regularly scheduled basis. The meeting ends with a reminder that the client can feel free to call the consultant at any time in the future, that development is a lifelong endeavor, and that the need for future support should be perceived not as a failure but as a tool for further growth. The consultant might also wish to share his/her appreciation for the opportunity to work with the client.

The expiration of contracted coaching hours may or may not coincide with the successful attainment of objectives, but it is another manner in which the process can end. One of the purposes of the contract is that it provides a target time frame for completion. As such, it may actually act as an impetus for the client to take more risks in experimenting with change while the consultant is still present; it may also be a way in which an unproductive coaching assignment may be terminated (see Chapter 14). When the end of the contract is approaching, the consultant reminds the client of the remaining hours. If the consultant believes that there is value in continuing the work, there is discussion about whether the client feels ready to end coaching. If the client wishes to continue, authorization is obtained, and the contract is amended to reflect updated time frames. If there is no perceived benefit in extending coaching, discussion focuses on what will be accomplished in the remaining time. The content of both the evaluation meeting with the client's manager and the final meeting centers on alternative developmental opportunities for the client.

The third way in which the coaching process may conclude is through early termination. When the consultant is an active participant in early termination, it is usually because he/she views the coaching as untenable because of an intractable system, client, or process (see Chapter 14). The suggestion that coaching should end is made to the client, with the reasons why. If the client agrees, together the consultant and client discuss the most appropriate way to conclude; if the client does not agree, the very act of suggesting termination may prove to be an effective intervention (see Chapter 13). When, on the other hand, the consultant is surprised by early termination, it is usually because something has abruptly changed (e.g., the client has been terminated or suddenly leaves the organization, the client's sponsor changes and will not support coaching, etc.). The consultant may attempt to contact the client for a final meeting but may be forced to accept the finality of the situation as it exists. In addition, there are times when the client terminates abruptly—either by discussing it with the consultant or by consistently canceling appointments or refusing to return calls. Perhaps he/she finds the coaching process too difficult, does not believe it is possible to change, simply does not relate well to the consultant, or, in the case of seemingly successful work and a strong alliance, the ending process is too painful. Here, it is absolutely essential that the consultant attempt to engage the client in discussion to determine if this is an indirect plea for help, a predicable form of resistance, or a legitimate desire to disengage from a nonproductive endeavor. If the client refuses to meet, the consultant is forced to accept the finality of the situation.

What must never be underestimated in any of these cases is the impact on both the client and the consultant. Strong alliances and successful outcomes make for poignant conclusions, unsuccessful outcomes cause disappointment and regret, and early terminations can be frustrating and perplexing. During the conclusion of coaching, in whatever form, the consultant must be ever vigilant to the need to manage strong emotions—both the client's and his/her own.

THE CASE OF JEANNE (continued and concluded)

Jeanne started the session by reporting that she liked who she was becoming at work—a more tolerant, kinder person. She was making a conscious effort to pause to consider alternatives before making decisions, particularly when she felt herself under pressure for a quick response. She described several instances in which she had told colleagues that she would have to think about what she had heard and would get back to them, as well as several examples of allowing her subordinates to generate their own alternatives and decisions while she coached them through the process. She said she had realized that it was not only more effective but also more efficient to allow others the time to make their own decisions and to allow herself the time to be objective in her decision making. She also mentioned that she had discovered how important it was to take some time for herself each day, and had begun to awaken a half hour earlier than her family to take time to be alone with her thoughts. At the end of the meeting, she asked for advice on how to sustain what she was feeling and how to channel some of the frustrations that she knew would continue to arise. We talked about things that had been pleasurable for her in the past, and she decided to become involved with a regular running and yoga regimen. When I reminded her that, based on the contractual agreement, we should be preparing to conclude our work, she told me that she was not yet ready. Despite my assurance that she no longer needed me, she was visibly relieved when we agreed that she would request her manager's approval to extend our work together. We scheduled our next meeting for 3 weeks later.

Her manager readily agreed and called me to confirm the extension but wanted me to know that he already considered the coaching assignment a great success, enumerating the ways in which he had seen changes in Jeanne's behavior. I asked him if he had had that discussion with her, and he assured me that he would schedule a time to do so.

That next meeting did, in fact, turn out to be our last. When I entered the room, Jeanne stood, came from behind her desk, and hugged me. She sat and said, "Well, I don't really have anything troubling me. Things are still crazy here, but I feel in control and relaxed." I told her that I was delighted but not surprised. I again suggested that we had completed our work together. This time she agreed, telling me that she had already met with her manager and that he, too, agreed that her objectives had been met. Without being prompted, she summarized how she felt, giving specific examples. First, she no longer felt overwhelmed. She was now able to say no to work requested by the president "even if it takes a day to think about how to say it." She was able to do "good enough" rather than perfect work on some things. She was better able to confront issues with her staff as they happened. She found herself able to "pick my battles." She found herself being easier on herself and wasn't using "stupid" to describe herself to herself any longer—or was at least aware of how often she had done so in the past. She was able to be patient to do things right, even if it meant delaying some of them. She was taking walks with her son, running, and going to yoga regularly. And, most important, she felt able to show her humanity—even giving herself permission to "lose it" occasionally and quickly apologize. She concluded by sharing her feelings about the process: "It was incremental. You allowed me to go at my own pace, and I never felt like I was falling off a cliff. You also helped me to see what I couldn't change: 'This is the organization. This is you. You can learn to cope with what exists, rather than trying to force the situation to change.' And one of the neatest parts of this is that I've been working with someone with whom I'd like to be friends." Before leaving, I told Jeanne that she could feel free to call me if she needed me again—and that doing so was not a failure. As I rose, she hugged me for a second time, and we said good-bye. As I left the building, I knew that I was experiencing both joy and pain—the simultaneous emotions that come from letting go.

ANALYSIS: THE CASE OF JEANNE

In this case, it was clear to the consultant, and reinforced by the conversation with the client's manager, that the client had achieved her objectives within the time parameters of the contract. The client, however, did not feel confident enough to proceed on her own. Simply the knowledge that the time could be extended allowed her the freedom to continue to experiment with her new behaviors. As she did so, something new occurred—her behaviors became self-correcting and self-reinforcing. Once she was able to nonjudgmentally self-reflect on her behaviors and their outcomes, she became her own coach. In doing so, moreover, she was able to do the same for her staff and in her interactions with her manager. She had internalized the very essence of the coaching process and no longer needed an external coach.

PART III

Multidimensional Executive Coaching: Practical Considerations

If we do not try to think through in advance the ethical implications of commitments we make, we are bound to get trapped into actions dictated by expediency. In this way, we can lose the trust of people in the field and even come to mistrust ourselves.

—William Foote Whyte (1984)

CHAPTER 14

Identifying Potential Coaching Failures: When to Decline or Exit a Coaching Engagement

Even the most effective of executive consulting processes cannot counteract three factors that, taken together or separately, are virtually guaranteed to result in consulting failures: (1) a client who is unwilling and/or unable to change, (2) an organization that is unwilling and/or unable to support the coaching process, and (3) a consultant who is an inappropriate match for the client and/or the client system. Knowing when to decline a potential coaching engagement or exit from an existing one is a critical consulting skill, and this chapter is written in an effort to help consultants identify those situations.

FACTORS IN THE CLIENT

The Client Does Not See the Need to Change

This happens quite frequently when coaching is foisted on the client by well-intentioned others. Frequently, a client's manager has been unsuccessful in addressing a developmental need with the client, or a human resources group desires to provide coaching throughout the organization. If the client is not motivated, however, the coaching process will be futile.

> Example: A senior manager was asked to work with me as part of a leadership training program for the top 100 executives in the company. He informed me that he had no need for coaching, had been successful doing exactly what he was doing for 30 years, and had seen training programs come and go. Despite my best efforts

to discuss his identified developmental needs, the client was not interested in engaging in the effort.

The Client Is Not Capable of Changing

Self-reflection is a fundamental requirement for change. When a client lacks the capacity or desire to observe his/her own actions and their impact and consequences, coaching cannot be successful. Most frequently, there are two causes for the incapacity to self-reflect: character disorders and/or rigid defense mechanisms. When an individual suffers from a narcissistic personality disorder or a psychopathic personality disorder, there is an absence of an observing ego (the ability to observe oneself) and/or a well-functioning superego (the center of moral fiber and conscience). If a client suffers from either of these disorders, no matter how highly functioning he or she may be, coaching is doomed to failure. When any client consistently defends against self-reflection through the rigid use of denial, splitting, distortion, projection, or projective identification, coaching cannot be successful.

> Example: A department head had alienated all of his peers by the time his manager asked me to work with him. The client expressed complete willingness to engage in coaching but assured me I would discover that the only real problem was that he was smarter and more competent than everyone around him. Throughout the feedback, objective setting, and coaching, he agreed to put into practice everything I suggested, did none of it, and continued to vehemently attack the actions of those around him.

The Client Has Ulterior Motives for Engaging in Coaching

When a client engages in coaching for any other reason than to change his/her own behavior, coaching will fail. Some of these reasons are to appease someone else, to prove that someone else is to blame, or to gain status or attention.

> Example: A client's peer, who previously had been part of the client's 360-degree interview process, made repeated requests to her manager for her own coaching. When the latter finally agreed and I began the process, this new client was extremely motivated. The feedback session, however, greatly upset her. She did not know that she had any developmental needs, and when they were identified, she threatened to leave the organization.

FACTORS IN THE ORGANIZATION

Lack of Support for the Client

If relevant others, especially the client's manager, do not support the client, it is impossible to appropriately contract, to engage in assessment and objectives setting, and ultimately, to sustain change. This lack of support can take many forms—insufficient financial resources, limited time, incomplete information, or outright refusal to be of help—but all seriously jeopardize the coaching success.

> Example: A new client was very eager to begin coaching, and a day after our initial meeting, she had prepared the interview list and contacted all those individuals on it. It took 6 months to complete the interviews: Several individuals were difficult to reach and did not return e-mails or calls, a number of interviewees rescheduled three or four times, and one was called to a meeting 10 minutes before the scheduled time and could not be reached for another appointment. Many of the interviewees did not "feel comfortable" answering some questions.

Lack of Support for the Coaching Process

When a demand is made by the client organization that some aspect of the coaching process be eliminated or substantively modified, the assignment is at risk. Typically, these demands center on limiting or eliminating entirely the qualitative interview process, sharing confidential information, or changing the scope of the work.

> Example: The head of organizational development for a large corporation asked to meet with me to discuss my approach to coaching. After I described the details of my approach to her, she informed me that the organization had developed its own 360-degree instrument and did not believe in paying consultants to do redundant work. She also informed me that the company only hired coaches who met with representatives of her department and clients' managers on a monthly basis to review the client's status and evaluate the client's progress in meeting the stated objectives.

Abrogation of Managerial Responsibilities

It is all too commonly the case that a manager lacks either the skill or the inclination to address performance issues and arranges for a coach to do that work with someone who reports to him/her. In this situation, the pressing need for coaching is not with the identified client but with the manager.

> Example: The human resources director of a client organization called to request that I work with a department head whose manager had "given up" on him. I asked why, and the director responded with a long list of the manager's complaints. When I asked if the manager had discussed these with the prospective client, I was told that the manager did not like to confront unpleasant issues.

Ulterior Motives

An organization can attempt to use coaching for inappropriate reasons, such as assessing the client for promotion, finding justification to terminate the client, or avoiding litigation. Coaching is a vehicle for a client's development; using it for any other purpose is highly inadvisable and puts the client, the consultant, and the organization itself at risk.

> Example: The executive director of a large nonprofit agency asked me to work with the head of its most high-profile department. During my meeting with the prospective client, the director called and asked that I stop by his office before leaving. When I did so, he told me that he wanted to know my assessment of the client. I told him that I could not share that information with him, but that I thought I could work with the client. The director became visibly agitated and told me that he had to determine whether he should terminate the client and that he needed my opinion as quickly as possible. When I explained that if that was what he required, he would be better served hiring a consultant who specialized in management assessment, he became quite angry and told me that he, too, was the client.

Unconscious Group Dynamics

Group-as-a-whole forces often result in clients unconsciously taking up roles on behalf of a group. If the forces are powerful enough, they will undermine any attempts by the client to reject the role and concomitantly to change behavior.

> Example: My client, a highly respected, admired, and very outspoken executive within a national not-for-profit institution, had encountered some difficulties dealing with the new president. She had realized, through our coaching, that she was being used by her peer group to disagree with the president when no one else would speak up. She practiced remaining silent when issues arose so that others

would address them. Within a short period of time, she became the repeated target of her peer group's anger and blame.

Unconscious Systemic Forces

When an organization is in denial about its pernicious systemic issues (e.g., racial, gender, religious, or ethnic biases; illegal practices; power and authority abuses; etc.) and a client is enmeshed in them, there is little chance that coaching can be successful.

> Example: In the same week, I was contacted by two different managers from an organization in the midst of a gender-based class action suit. Each of the managers, both male, had identified a female direct report in his group who needed coaching. The first female executive was considered too aggressive in her manner—she was described as intimidating and authoritarian. The second was considered too weak—she was described as too collaborative and polite.

Constant Organizational Turmoil

When an organization is in continuous flux, when structural and personnel changes are constant, and when there is perpetual instability, there is no relevant context in which coaching can occur. When a client faces the probability of constantly shifting roles, expectations, reporting lines, and relationships, coaching becomes the vehicle with which to deal with keeping the self intact rather than a planned program of personal change.

> Example: While involved in coaching, a client received a much desired promotion. Two weeks later, his position was layered, and he found himself with curtailed responsibilities reporting to a former peer. Two months later, his original manager (with whom coaching objectives were defined) was terminated, and the former peer to whom he was currently reporting was transferred to a different division. He was assigned to another former peer who had had no exposure to him while he was engaged in his coaching work.

FACTORS IN THE CONSULTANT

Inappropriate Expertise

The term "executive coaching" has gradually taken on the broadest possible meaning, encompassing any support or assistance that a manager receives from any other individual, internal or external. It is therefore imperative that consultants who provide executive coaching services be clear about their particular areas of expertise. For example, a management consultant whose expertise is finance is not prepared to coach a manager who is having interpersonal difficulty, nor is a psychologist with no training in business prepared to assist a manager with marketing strategy. Just as important is the delineation of the hierarchical level with which a consultant works most effectively. Working with CEOs to improve their performance is substantively different from working with first-line managers.

> Example: The president of a small company, pleased with the progress he saw in the three vice presidents whom he had asked me to coach, called to request that I work with his administrative assistant. He described her difficulty as "imperiousness" with the other administrative staff and the need for her to understand the impact of her behavior on her peers.

Inappropriate Group Memberships

The group memberships of the consultant must be appropriate for both the client and the client organization. If the consultant's identity or organizational group memberships do not facilitate the process, coaching cannot succeed.

> Example: I received a call from the human resources director of a corporation to which I had not previously consulted. She asked me to do "on-boarding" for the new head of a subsidiary and explained that he would probably need support because he was much younger than his peers and direct reports, did not understand the politics of the organization, and would be the only African-American on the executive committee. She added that this would be a great way to bring me into the company.

Ulterior Motives

There are a host of reasons why consultants accept questionable coaching assignments, ranging from supplementing income to business development to the need to rescue the client or client organization to association with a prestigious group to the challenge of achieving what others see as impossible. If the central concern for an assignment is not the client and what is required to help improve his/her performance, including a deliberate and coherent plan, the effort cannot succeed.

> Example: I received an urgent call from a former client organization with a request to work with a management team whose staff was

complaining to human resources of racial and ethnic discrimination. I was told they had tried to resolve the issue internally, then turned to the human resources department, and now believed that I was the only one who could save the situation. It was critical to start work immediately to avoid the escalation of the grievance and further disruption to the working environment.

Personal Triggers

A consultant is not free of unconscious emotional reactions to powerful psychological stimuli. Knowing what those triggers are, how intensely they impact effectiveness, and when to walk away from situations in which they are present are the consultant's ethical and moral obligations.

> Example: When I met a client, my immediate reaction was a strong aversion to him. As the meeting progressed, I realized how much he reminded me of a former manager who was manipulative, erratic, and abusive. When I left the meeting, I felt no empathy for the client.

Going Native

Consultants must guard against becoming so enmeshed in an organization that it is impossible to maintain their own external perspective and boundaries, without which the client cannot be successfully coached.

> Example: After 2 years of coaching highly paid senior executives within a high-status corporation, I was becoming increasingly dissatisfied with what I had achieved in life and began to question whether I had been wise to change careers. When I read newspapers with critical comments about the company, I found myself feeling defensive and angry at the writer.

IDENTIFYING POTENTIAL FAILURES

The most difficult aspect of identifying potential coaching failures is differentiating resistance from intractability and what is situational from what is characterological. In addition, the signals often do not make themselves entirely clear until well into the process. Exiting becomes quite different depending on the particular stage of the coaching process, and while the entry stage is the easiest to exit, it is usually the most difficult in which to identify potential failures. Unless the client explicitly rejects coaching, the client's organization blatantly refuses to support the process, or the consultant feels unmitigated antipathy toward the individual or the organization, it is very hard to judge whether coaching will be unsuccessful. Even in the case of a client who appears character-disordered, it is often much too early to determine whether the characteristic behavior is situationally induced.

If there are early warnings of unusual obstacles, however, the consultant can prepare for a timely exit by limiting the scope of the initial engagement. By contracting only through feedback and objective setting, the consultant is able to repeatedly enter the organization, meet with relevant others, and conduct the feedback session. Much more data is available as a result, and, if the determination is made at this point that coaching cannot be successful, the consultant can complete the contractual obligation and exit, avoiding the pain and possible stigma of early termination.

There are, of course, situations in which coaching failures cannot be avoided. These can often provide the consultant with the greatest learning opportunities and can be instrumental in helping the consultant prevent similar experiences in the future. The reader may rest assured that many of the examples given in the earlier sections of this chapter fall into this category.

ANNOTATED BIBLIOGRAPHY

Kahn, W. A. (1993). Facilitating and undermining organizational change. *Journal of Applied Behavioral Science, 29,* 32–55.
  An award-winning article about the factors in the consultant that, if unexamined, can undermine the success of an organizational intervention.
McWilliams, N. (1994). *Psychoanalytic diagnosis.* New York: Guildford Press.
  Of particular relevance are the sections on defensive processes (chapters 5–6) and the holistic presentation of psychopathic and narcissistic personalities (chapters 7–8).
Mirvis, P. H., & Berg, D. N. (1977). *Failures in organization development and change.* New York: Wiley-Interscience.
  Describes consultation failures at several stages in the change process and in a broad range of organizational settings, as well as what each author learned from the failure.

CHAPTER 15

Implications for Practice

The practice of executive coaching is not, of course, without implications. Working within an organization, in and of itself, presents certain challenges. Furthermore, using the multidimensional coaching process, with its emphasis on the excavation of unconscious forces, the simultaneity of multidimensional interventions, and the consultant's use of the self, presents additional layers of complexity. Some of the most significant implications are discussed in this chapter.

EDUCATION AND TRAINING

Perhaps the most obvious implication is the education and training of executive coaches. While discussion within the field is expanding, there is, as yet, no definitive position on what constitutes adequate preparation for this challenging and demanding work. Even the most cursory review of the contents of this book, however, indicates that executive coaching requires an imposing depth and breadth. It requires a comprehensive knowledge of psychology—clinical and organizational, individual and group. It requires a thorough understanding of management practices and the issues that senior leaders must confront on a daily basis. It requires the ability to maneuver through the peculiar labyrinths of diverse organizations—corporate, nonprofit, government, and educational. And it requires a deep awareness of one's self and the abiding commitment to continuous self-reflection and self-scrutiny. Table 15.1 is an outline of recommended topics for those who wish to be appropriately prepared to practice executive coaching in the manner suggested throughout this book.

COACHING VERSUS THERAPY

A second implication arises from competent utilization of psychological principles and techniques and the concomitant gray area that can emerge

TABLE 15.1.   Education and Training of Executive Coaches

Component 1: Psychological theory (individual)
- Psychodynamic theory
- Cognitive-behavioral theory
- Personality theory
- Adult development
- Adult learning
- Change theory

Component 2: Organizational psychology
- Role theory
- Group dynamics
- Intergroup dynamics
- Systems theory
- Nature of leadership and authority
- Change theory

Component 3: Management theory and practice
- Organizational structures
- Organizational behavior
- Leadership models
- Strategic planning
- Financial management
- Marketing principles
- Human resources management
- Performance management

Component 4: Practice skills
- Contracting
- Interviewing
- Observation
- Individual and organizational assessment
- Feedback
- Individual and group interventions
- Individual and group facilitation
- Outcome evaluation
- Use of self as tool

Component 5: Research methodology
- Qualitative research
- Quantitative research

(Continued)

PART IV

Multidimensional Executive Coaching: Bringing It All Together

We are concerned here with a new questioning, a new—and yet age-old—field of psychological experience.

—Carl G. Jung (1934/53)

CHAPTER 17

The Case of Margaret: A Multidimensional Analysis

THEORETICAL ANALYSIS

The broad systemic messages with which the client was being bombarded were evident from the very start. The initial contact from the president had demonstrated not only the organization's considerable esteem for the client but also the high expectations that were being demanded of her—"prominent," "highly visible," "most intellectually stimulating," all gave voice to an elitism that appeared to be surrounding the client and her role. This was underscored as the consultant arrived at the imposing entryway and impressive residence that housed the client's work site—a façade that belied the absence of barriers and guideposts to physical entry. The consultant's gothic imaginings, together with her relief upon locating the client, heightened the sense of underboundedness and led to the formulation of the first hypothesis: The client, despite her celebrity, was indeed feeling psychologically lost in a new role in a highly underbounded system and, consequently, needed someone who would help her find her way.

The client's forthright and unpretentious description of the issues gave ample evidence for the corroboration of the first hypothesis and crystallized the additional multiplicity of forces with which she was grappling: at the intergroup level, dynamics involving gender and expertise (heightened by the questioned value of the new unit); at the group level, the schism between research and administration (compounded by its parallels at the departmental level and by the client's conflicted feelings about giving up her own research); at the interpersonal level, the strained relationships with her assistant and the executive vice president; and at the individual level, her paralyzing inability to deal with anger. The apparent interaction of these forces led to the generation of two additional hypotheses: that the client's fear of anger was both cause and effect in the complex dynamics in which she was entangled, and that given the nature of existing intergroup dynamics, the consultant's gender and expertise would be the most salient of her group memberships in developing a strong working alliance with the client.

There were two significant data points that emerged from the three-way meeting. The first, of course, was the intensity of the client's negative feelings about her colleague; the second was her assertiveness, bordering on aggressiveness, with her senior manager. The consultant observed, firsthand, that the client was, in fact, quite capable of confrontation—at least with some individuals. Consequently, the consultant was convinced that the client's feelings about her colleague—and the unconscious forces triggering them—needed to be explored more deeply later in the coaching process.

The opportunity for that exploration presented itself, and was taken, in the very first coaching meeting. What turned out to be revelatory to the client was not simply the cause of her reaction (she had, after all, previously identified it in the course of therapy), but the fact that it influenced her behavior at work as well as in her personal life. Once articulated, the client quickly integrated the insight, and, with the added reinforcement of relevant information that the consultant had obtained during the course of the assessment interviews, the client was able to take giant leaps in confronting issues with her staff and capably managing her group. That the consultant had taken the opportunity to probe so deeply early in the process, that the client responded so readily, and that the consultant's emotions on behalf of the client were so accessible were testimony to the strength of the alliance that was forming between the two women. The elephant-in-the-room analogy, meant to distinguish coaching from therapy, was therefore not a random imaginative thought; it was the result of a powerful countertransference that enabled the consultant to plumb her own unconscious in order to respond to the client's intrapsychic needs. Initially expressed as a symbol of psychological impediment, it became, as was soon made clear, an archetypal representation of a powerful, protective matriarchal[1] figure—one that, in this context, would be neither abusive nor blaming as the client continued to confront the debilitating family-of-origin dynamics being triggered by the multilevel forces surrounding her. Furthermore, the intervention, served yet another purpose: By explicitly differentiating between coaching and therapy, the consultant was performing an overt act

[1] For additional information on the archetypal mother, see Jung, C. G. (1969). The concept of the collective unconscious. In *The archetypes and the collective unconscious (Collected Works, 9i*, pp. 42–53) (R. F. C. Hull, Trans.). Princeton: Princeton University Press. (Original work published 1936.)

client's self-defeating behavior. The homework assignment was a cognitive one—self-reflection.

The second meeting demonstrated that the client had taken her homework assignment quite seriously. Her self-reflection had led to awareness of a significant behavioral weakness and its source. The consultant's ability to draw on confirming feedback data, the use of positive reinforcement, the emergence of analogy and metaphor, and the role modeling of boundary management laid the groundwork for the third meeting and the ensuing plan to confront the client's direct report. Its successful execution at the fourth meeting was, in no small measure, related to the consultant's presence in the room (reminiscent of the elephant metaphor) during the dyadic event. This intervention was facilitated not only by the alliance with the client, but also by the relationship forged between the consultant and the direct report during the feedback interview.

The client's update at the fifth meeting demonstrated her integration of the new behavior. The consultant now articulated the concept of boundary management as a way in which to reinforce the client's success and to help her conceptualize the continuation of her homework—ongoing practice of the behavior with her staff. In many ways, then, the sixth meeting was a replication of the fifth, consisting of the client's update, positive reinforcement from the consultant, discussion about boundary management, and a related homework assignment. Because the homework seemed straightforward to the consultant, she had not anticipated the client's resistance. Consequently, when it surfaced, the consultant consciously employed use of self as a tool, carefully noting her reactions and thoughts as data that she could reference later in coaching.

The conclusion of the seventh meeting had been preceded by two unequivocally positive events—the enthusiastically received staff meeting and the affirming feedback report. Although the consultant had expected the remainder of this meeting to consist of the analysis of factors that had contributed to the success, she was prepared, as a result of the use of self as a tool in the former meeting, with what she considered to be an effective intervention for the client's continued resistance to managing her task boundaries—building self-confidence through self-reinforcement.

The ineffectiveness of both that intervention and its intended purpose became starkly apparent at the next meeting. An unexpected by-product, however, was its value in intensifying the client's resistance. When the consultant attempted, and failed, to reduce it with a cognitive technique (i.e., challenging negative thoughts), she returned to the homework assignment, still believing the appropriate intervention to be one that would raise the client's self-esteem. It, too, had just the opposite effect. Ultimately, it was the consultant's use of self as a tool that proved to be the effective method; it led to the here-and-now intervention that finally penetrated the resistance, making clear the anxiety that the client felt not only about lack of perfection but also pride in achievement. The consultant could then begin to grasp the meaning of the transference and understand, through the countertransference, the magnitude of the intrapsychic forces.

The consultant's planned intervention for the ninth meeting, therefore, was to suggest a return to therapy. It proved entirely unnecessary, as demonstrated by the client's affect, update, and self-analysis. The consultant identified her countertransference during this meeting as a reflection of the client's positive internal state and gave voice to it in a single statement of praise. The client was now ready to accept it.

In the remaining three sessions, the consultant simply served as a sounding board for the work that the client was doing on her own. Nothing more than observation, active listening, and positive reinforcement was required.

PRACTICE ISSUES

Four practice issues were salient throughout this case. The first and most evident was the maintenance of the boundary between coaching and therapy. The second was the impact of use of self as a tool on the consultant and the consultation. The third was maintaining confidentiality while engaging in a dyadic intervention. The fourth was the training and education required for a successful consultation.

The need for the consultant to be ever-vigilant to the boundary between coaching and therapy was extraordinarily critical in this case. There were a number of elements that made it so. Unconscious intrapsychic forces, family-of-origin dynamics, defense mechanisms, resistance, and concomitant psychodynamic interventions all played an unusually prominent role in this case. To add to the considerable power of those factors, there was the systemic pull, in the form of a highly underbounded organization, toward the collapsing of boundaries, which, in turn, influenced the ability of the client to establish them for herself and her group. The ability of the consultant to maintain the coaching boundaries was therefore not only an ethical imperative, it was the manner in which she gathered critical data about the organization and the client and, in turn, became the vehicle for some of the most pivotal interventions and insights in the case.

Appendix A. Sample Contracts

APPENDIX A-1

SAMPLE CONTRACT: FULL COACHING PROJECT

Date

Name
Company
Address

Dear (Authorizing Individual):

This will serve as the **Letter of Agreement** for the executive coaching to be conducted with (Name of Client). The preliminary coaching plan, based on initial discussion with (Client), is enclosed.

Consulting fees of $xxx per hour are based on an estimated xx hours, for a total of $xxxx. Should it become necessary to exceed that estimate for any reason, no work will be done without prior approval. Fees will be billed twice—after the feedback session and at the conclusion of the individual coaching sessions outlined in the plan—and will include total hours incurred up to each point.

As we have discussed, all information shared by individuals during the interview process will be treated confidentially and will be used only to develop a profile for (Client). The latter will be discussed with her in a private feedback meeting and will not be available to any other individual. In addition, all discussions with (Client) will be handled with complete confidentiality.

Please indicate your authorization to proceed by signing a copy of this document where indicated below and returning it to me at your earliest convenience. Should you have any questions, please feel free to contact me.

I am looking forward to working with (Client) and (Name of Organization), and I thank you for the opportunity to do so.

Sincerely,

Approved:_____Date:_____

APPENDIX A-2

SAMPLE CONTRACT: PHASED COACHING PROJECT
WITH TRAVEL REQUIREMENTS

Date

Name
Company
Address

Dear (Authorizing Individual):

This will serve as the **Letter of Agreement** for the executive coaching to be conducted with (Name of Client). The preliminary coaching plan, based on initial discussion with (Client) and proposed in two phases is enclosed.

Phase I consulting fees of $xxx per hour are based on an estimated xx hours, for a total of $xxxx, exclusive of travel expenses. Should it become necessary to exceed that estimate for any reason, no work will be done without prior approval. Phase II fees and hours will be estimated once specific coaching objectives are defined, and a separate letter of agreement will be submitted prior to proceeding. Fees will be billed at the conclusion of each phase of the program and will include actual consulting hours and related travel expense incurred up to each point.

As we have discussed, all information shared by individuals during the interview process will be treated confidentially and will be used only to develop a profile for (Client). The latter will be discussed with him in a private feedback meeting and will not be available to any other individual. In addition, all discussions with (Client) will be handled with complete confidentiality.

Please indicate your authorization to proceed by signing a copy of this document where indicated below and returning it to me at your earliest convenience. Should you have any questions, please feel free to contact me.

Sincerely,

Approved:_____Date:_____

Appendix C.
Sample 360-Degree
Interview Protocols

SAMPLE 360-DEGREE INTERVIEW PROTOCOL:
GENERIC MANAGEMENT SKILLS

Client: _____

Interviewee: _____

Date: _____

(Introduction: Purpose, Confidentiality, Timing, Questions)

1. How long have you known _____? In what capacity?

2. How often do you interact with _____ ? For what purpose(s)?

3. Please describe _____'s role as you understand it.

4. How would you describe _____'s management style? Is it consistent with what is expected for the role? Explain. (What would be the appropriate style for the position?)

5. Please comment on his/her effectiveness in the following areas (please give examples):

   • Planning/organizational skills

   • Delegation

   • Communication

   • Motivational skills (i.e., ability to motivate others)

   • Leadership skills

   • Interpersonal skills

6. How comfortable are you working with _____? What is the best thing about working with ____? What would you change about working with _____?

7. Have you learned anything from _____?

8. If you were to give _____ advice, what would it be?

9. If you were making the hiring decision for _____'s job, would you hire _____? Why or why not?

10. Is there anything that wasn't asked that should have been (i.e., anything else it would be helpful to know)?

APPENDIX C-2

SAMPLE 360-DEGREE INTERVIEW PROTOCOL: CUSTOMIZED LEADERSHIP SKILLS

Client: _____

Interviewee:_____

Date: _____

(Introduction: Purpose, Confidentiality, Timing, Questions, Examples)

1. How long have you known _____? In what capacity?

2. How often do you interact with _____? For what purpose(s)?

3. How would you describe _____ as a leader?

4. How would you rate his/her planning skills?

   • How has she/he exhibited his/her commitment to the strategic plan?

   • To what extent does his/her planning consider the rest of the organization?

5. How would you rate the overall quality of the people reporting to him/her?

   • How does he/she motivate them?

   • How does he/she develop them?

   • How does he/she hold them accountable?

6. How does _____ interact with customers, both internal and external?

7. To what degree to you consider _____ an expert in his/her area?

8. How effective is his/her decision making?

9. How flexible is he/she?

10. To what extent do you think _____ is aware of his/her impact on others?

11. How comfortable are you working with _____? What is the best thing about working with ____? What would you change about working with _____?

12. If you could give _____ advice, what would it be?

13. Is there anything that wasn't asked that should have been (i.e., anything else it would be helpful to know)?

COMPLEX AREAS (continued)

Interpersonal
- Fun/sense of humor
- Caring/human
- Personable
- Well respected

- Quick temper/outbursts
- Shows frustration
- Moodiness *("I have to pick the times I can tell him something.")*
- Impatient/intolerant of others' ideas *("He doesn't suffer fools well.")*
- Defensive/confrontational/reactive: *"He should ask questions/ask for input before jumping into action." "He's the boss. He doesn't have to get to their level. He doesn't have to react right away."*
- Aggressive/*"tough"*

MOST COMMON ADVICE

1. **Keep balance in your life.** *("Slow down and enjoy where you are; make time for your family.")*

2. **"Pick your battles."**

3. **Think about running a business rather than a staff group** *("latter not challenging enough").*

4. **Be in the office more** *("versus task forces, committees, etc.").*

5. **"Keep doing what you're doing. You're terrific."**

APPENDIX D-2

SAMPLE FEEDBACK REPORT: CLIENT B (ALL COMPLEX)

EXECUTIVE COACHING FEEDBACK

Client B

CONFIDENTIAL

EXECUTIVE COACHING FEEDBACK
Client B

ORGANIZATIONAL CONTEXT

- Organizational culture

  -"We're Number 1"
  -Relational/collaborative
  -Respect for authority
  -Difficult for "outsiders"

- Competition/territoriality at the top

- Perceived tension among peers

ROLE EXPECTATIONS

- Head of group

- Strategic partner

- Thought leader

- *"Big, broad role"*

MANAGEMENT SKILLS SET

Planning and Organization
- Prepared/thinks things through
- Well-thought-out insights
- Proactive
- *"Solid vision of where to take organization"*
- *"Grasps issues and lays down structure"*
- *"Have seen him step in and resolve chaos and build a working team"*

- Lack of clarity and focus
  -Many changes in direction without explanation
  -Frenetic/reactive
  -Uneven
- Execution gap
  -Plan not accomplished
  -Lack of delivery
  -Work done without results: *"Paralysis by analysis"*

Delegation
- Clear expectations
- Knows what and to whom to delegate

- Micromanages
- Tasks but not responsibility
- *"Sometimes it's preferable not to think on your own because if it differs from his view; you'll have to redo it."*

Motivation
- Enthusiastic
- Positive
- Respectful
- Empowering
- Public praise

Feedback—Client B
Page 3

- High expectations
- Results based

- *"Fixated on getting things done, not how. The toll he extracts is significant in terms of emotional energy and team spirit."*
- *Formal authority:* *"He would benefit by being less directive and condescending and getting people involved in setting objectives."*
- *"Positions himself as the key player; always trying to be front and center"*

Communication
- Precise/succinct/clear: *"chooses words carefully"*
- Straightforward/no hidden agenda
- Articulate
- Listens

- Condescending/patronizing
- *"Listens but does not hear"*
- *"Does not identify audience"*
- Cuts people off: *"no opportunity for full distillation of ideas"*
- *"Misses nuances of others' reactions"*

Interpersonal
- Warm/nice/thoughtful
- Well intentioned
- Charming/personable/interesting
- Light hearted/sense of humor

- Cold/stiff/uncomfortable/guarded: *"hard to get to know"*
- Combative/opinionated/stubborn: *"draws his line and then is very hard"*
- Off-putting/dismissive: *"doesn't know or care about his impact on others"*

Leadership
- Intelligent: *"keen mind"*
- Knowledgeable/knows and understands business
- Insightful

- Creative
- Strong senior presence
- Enormous capacity for work

- Militaristic/hierarchical: *"gets things done by telling people what to do"*
- Self-promoting *"moves own agenda at expense of others"; "defects account-ability, blames others, takes credit"*

MOST COMMON ADVICE

People Management

- *Show more trust and delegation in team; empower them more. Give them more latitude and responsibility.*

- *Be sensitive to what matters to people and be clear about criteria.*

- *More focus on coaching and developing—group would be more effective with each other and the organization.*

- *Once in a while, take a walk around; pop head into offices. Be a presence in the office.*

- *Strive for focus. Clearly set mission and priorities; articulate clearly around these. Let people rise to them and then give them credit.*

Collaboration

- *Demonstrate that an exchange of opinions is valuable.*

- *Be more open to others' ideas/input, not just your own. You could leverage this and not repeat work.*

- *Learn to negotiate. Give up something when it is not important to you but is to others.*

Appendix E.
Sample Organic Questionnaire

EXECUTIVE COACHING EVALUATION

Dear Evaluator:

The purpose of this study is to discover the effects, if any, of executive coaching on the behaviors of those who undergo the process. Therefore, your perceptions in the present and the past are crucial to the research.

This evaluation has three sections:

- Section I asks you to reflect on your interactions with NAME approximately 12–18 months ago and to describe her professional behavior at that time.

- Section II contains a series of statements about *past* behaviors. Some apply to xxxx, and some apply to others who have undergone coaching but not to her. You are asked to indicate the extent to which you agree or disagree with each.

- Section III asks you to reflect on your current interactions with xxxx and to describe her professional behavior at the present time.

- Section III contains the same statements about *present* behaviors. Again, some apply to xxxx and some apply to others but not her; and you are asked to indicate the extent to which you agree or disagree with each.

Thank you very much for participating in this study.

Evaluation—Section I

Directions: Please reflect on your interactions with xxxx approximately *one year to eighteen months ago.* In the space below, briefly describe what xxxx was like as a professional. Then please answer the questions in the following sections.

Evaluation—Section II

Directions: Please indicate to what extent you agree or disagree with the following statements about xxxx as they describe her behavior approximately 12–18 months ago. Please place a check mark in the appropriate box.

Key:

1. Disagree completely
2. Disagree somewhat
3. Neither agree nor disagree
4. Agree somewhat
5. Agree completely

		1	2	3	4	5
1.	She demonstrated strong organizational skills.	☐	☐	☐	☐	☐
2.	She was warm and kind in our dealings.	☐	☐	☐	☐	☐
3.	She was easily overwhelmed.	☐	☐	☐	☐	☐
4.	She tried to do too many things at one time.	☐	☐	☐	☐	☐
5.	She was adept at handling difficult situations with staff.	☐	☐	☐	☐	☐
6.	She had her job under control.	☐	☐	☐	☐	☐
7.	I knew where I stood with her.	☐	☐	☐	☐	☐
8.	I experienced her as "abrupt."	☐	☐	☐	☐	☐
9.	I experienced her as "condescending."	☐	☐	☐	☐	☐
10.	She communicated clearly to me.	☐	☐	☐	☐	☐
11.	She demonstrated to me that it was important to achieve her goals.	☐	☐	☐	☐	☐
12.	I did not know what she expected of me.	☐	☐	☐	☐	☐
13.	She intimidated me.	☐	☐	☐	☐	☐
14.	She was a mentor to me.	☐	☐	☐	☐	☐

Evaluation—Section II (continued)

Key:

1.   Disagree completely
2.   Disagree somewhat
3.   Neither agree nor disagree
4.   Agree somewhat
5.   Agree completely

		1	2	3	4	5
15.	She kept me informed.	☐	☐	☐	☐	☐
16.	I rarely observed her delegating work.	☐	☐	☐	☐	☐
17.	I trusted her to keep a confidence.	☐	☐	☐	☐	☐
18.	I observed her overreacting to things when under stress.	☐	☐	☐	☐	☐
19.	I described her as "frantic."	☐	☐	☐	☐	☐
20.	She did not provide learning opportunities for employees.	☐	☐	☐	☐	☐
21.	I experienced her as overly focused and task-oriented.	☐	☐	☐	☐	☐
22.	She demonstrated a sense of urgency about her work.	☐	☐	☐	☐	☐
23.	She allowed me to make mistakes and helped me learn from them.	☐	☐	☐	☐	☐
24.	She confused me.	☐	☐	☐	☐	☐
25.	She inspired me to do my best work.	☐	☐	☐	☐	☐
26.	She made quick decisions that were not always the best ones.	☐	☐	☐	☐	☐
27.	I saw her as able to say "no" to certain things asked of her.	☐	☐	☐	☐	☐
28.	She rarely praised and recognized my work.	☐	☐	☐	☐	☐
29.	She abused the power of her position.	☐	☐	☐	☐	☐
30.	She preferred email to face-to-face communication.	☐	☐	☐	☐	☐

Evaluation—Section III

Directions: Please reflect on your interactions with xxxx *currently*. In the space below, briefly describe what xxxx is like as a professional. Then please answer the questions in the following sections.

Evaluation—Section IV

Directions: Please indicate to what extent you agree or disagree with the following statements about xxxx as they describe her behavior currently. Please place a check mark in the appropriate box.

Key:
1.   Disagree completely
2.   Disagree somewhat
3.   Neither agree nor disagree
4.   Agree somewhat
5.   Agree completely

		1	2	3	4	5
1.	I trust her to keep a confidence.	☐	☐	☐	☐	☐
2.	I experience her as "abrupt."	☐	☐	☐	☐	☐
3.	I experience her as focused and task-oriented.	☐	☐	☐	☐	☐
4.	She demonstrates to me that it is important to achieve her goals.	☐	☐	☐	☐	☐
5.	I describe her as "frantic."	☐	☐	☐	☐	☐
6.	I know where I stand with her.	☐	☐	☐	☐	☐
7.	I observe her overreacting to things when under stress.	☐	☐	☐	☐	☐
8.	She communicates clearly to me.	☐	☐	☐	☐	☐
9.	She demonstrates strong organizational skills.	☐	☐	☐	☐	☐
10.	She abuses the power of her position.	☐	☐	☐	☐	☐
11.	She allows me to make mistakes and helps me learn from them.	☐	☐	☐	☐	☐
12.	She is a mentor to me.	☐	☐	☐	☐	☐
13.	She intimidates me.	☐	☐	☐	☐	☐
14.	I rarely observe her delegating work.	☐	☐	☐	☐	☐

*Evaluation—**Section IV** (continued)*

Key:
1. Disagree completely
2. Disagree somewhat
3. Neither agree nor disagree
4. Agree somewhat
5. Agree completely

		1	2	3	4	5
15.	She demonstrates a sense of urgency about her work.	☐	☐	☐	☐	☐
16.	She inspires me to do my best work.	☐	☐	☐	☐	☐
17.	She has her job under control.	☐	☐	☐	☐	☐
18.	She does not provide learning opportunities for employees.	☐	☐	☐	☐	☐
19.	She confuses me.	☐	☐	☐	☐	☐
20.	She keeps me informed.	☐	☐	☐	☐	☐
21.	She makes quick decisions that are not always the best ones.	☐	☐	☐	☐	☐
22.	She rarely praises and recognizes my work.	☐	☐	☐	☐	☐
23.	She prefers email to face-to-face communication.	☐	☐	☐	☐	☐
24.	I see her as able to say "no" to certain things asked of her.	☐	☐	☐	☐	☐
25.	She tries to do too many things at one time.	☐	☐	☐	☐	☐
26.	I do not know what she expects of me.	☐	☐	☐	☐	☐
27.	She is adept at handling difficult situations with staff.	☐	☐	☐	☐	☐
28.	She is easily overwhelmed.	☐	☐	☐	☐	☐
29.	I experience her as "condescending".	☐	☐	☐	☐	☐
30.	She is warm and kind in our dealings.	☐	☐	☐	☐	☐

References

Alderfer, C. P. (1980a). Consulting to underbounded systems. In C. P. Alderfer & C. L. Cooper (Eds.), *Advances in experiential social processes* (Vol. 2, pp. 267–295). New York: John Wiley & Sons.

Alderfer, C. P. (1980b). The methodology of organizational diagnosis. *Professional Psychology, II* (3), 459–468.

Alderfer, C. P. (1986). An intergroup perspective on group dynamics. In J. Lorsch (Ed.), *Handbook of organizational behavior* (pp. 190–222). Englewood Cliffs, NJ: Prentice Hall.

Alderfer, C. P., & Brown, L. D. (1972). Designing an "empathic questionnaire" for organizational research. *Journal of Applied Psychology, 56,* 456–460.

Alderfer, C. P., & Brown, L. D. (1975). *Learning from changing: Organizational diagnosis and development.* Beverly Hills, CA: Sage.

American Psychological Association (2003). Ethical principles of psychologists and code of conduct. *American Psychologist, 57.*

Argyris, C. (1975). Introduction. In C. P. Alderfer & L. D. Brown, *Learning from changing: Organizational diagnosis and development* (pp. 1–6). Beverly Hills, CA: Sage.

Berg, D. N., & Smith, K. K. (1985). The clinical demands of research methods. In D. Berg & K. Smith (Eds.), *Exploring clinical methods for social research* (pp. 21–34). Beverly Hills, CA: Sage.

Bion, W. R. (1961). *Experiences in groups.* New York: Basic Books.

Brotman, L. E., & Liberi, W. P. (1998). Executive coaching: The need for standards of competence. *Consulting Psychology Journal, 50*(1), 40–46.

Cammann, C. (1985). Action usable knowledge. In D. Berg & K. Smith (Eds.), *Exploring clinical methods for social research* (pp. 109–122). Beverly Hills, CA: Sage.

Campbell, D. T., & Fiske, D. W. (1959). Convergent & discriminant validation by the multi-trait multi-method matrix. *Psychological Bulletin, 56,* 81–105.

Cernak, T. L., & Brown, S. (1982). Interactional group therapy with the adult children of alcoholics. *International Journal of Group Psychotherapy, 32*(3), 375–389.

Corporate therapy. (2003, November 23). *The Economist print edition,* 1–2.

Diedrich, R. C. (1996). An iterative approach to executive coaching. *Consulting Psychology Journal, 48*(2), 61–66.

Fairbairn, W. R. D. (1952). *Psychoanalytic studies of the personality.* London: Routledge & Kegan Paul.

Fancher, R. (1973). *Psychoanalytic psychology: The development of Freud's thought.* New York: W. W. Norton.

Ghent, E. (1989). Credo: The dialectics of one-person and two-person psychologies. *Contemporary Psychoanalysis, 25*(2), 169–211.

Greco, J. (2001). Hey, coach. *The Journal of Business Strategy, 22*, 28–31.

Judge, W. Q., & Cowell, J. (1996). The brave new world of executive coaching. *Business Horizons,* July-August, 71–77.

Jung, C. G. (1971). *The collected works of C. G. Jung: Vol. 6. Psychological Types* (R. F. C. Hull, Trans.). Princeton: Princeton University Press. (Original work published 1921).

Jung, C. G. (1953). *Two essays on analytical psychology.* (Collected Works, 7) (R. F. C. Hull, Trans.). Princeton: Princeton University Press. (Original work published 1934).

Kampa-Kokesch, S., & Anderson, M. Z. (2001). Executive coaching: A comprehensive review of the literature. *Consulting Psychology Journal, 53*(4), 205–228.

Kaplan, R. E., Drath, W. H., & Kofodimos, J. R. (1991). *Beyond ambition: How driven mangers can lead better and live better.* San Francisco, CA: Jossey-Bass.

Kiel, F., Rimmer, E., Williams, K., & Doyle, M. (1996). Coaching at the top. *Psychological Bulletin, 56*(2), 67–77.

Kilburg, R. R. (1996). Toward a conceptual understanding and definition of executive coaching. *Consulting Psychology Journal, 48*(2), 134–144.

Kilburg, R. R. (1997). Coaching and executive character: Core problems and basic approaches. *Consulting Psychology Journal, 49*(4), 281–299.

Kilburg, R. R. (2000). *Executive coaching: Developing managerial wisdom in a world of chaos.* Washington, DC: American Psychological Association.

Kohut, H. (1971). *The analysis of self: A systematic psychoanalytic approach to the treatment of narcissistic personality disorders.* New York: International Universities Press.

Levinson, D. J. (1959). Role, personality and social structure in the organizational setting. *Journal of Abnormal and Social Psychology, 58*, 170–180.

Levinson, D. J. (1978). *The seasons of a man's life.* New York: Knopf.

Levinson, H. (1996). Executive coaching. *Consulting Psychology Journal, 48*(2), 115–123.

Levinson, H., Molinari, J., & Spohn, A. G. (1972). *Organizational diagnosis.* Cambridge, MA: Harvard University Press.

McWilliams, N. (1994). *Psychoanalytic diagnosis.* New York: Guilford Press.

Miller, P.M., & Fagley, N. S. (1991). The effects of framing, problem variations, and providing rationale on choice. *Personality and Social Psychology Bulletin, 17*, 517–522.

Mitchell, S. A., & Black, M. J. (1995). *Freud and beyond.* New York: Basic Books.

Orenstein, R. L. (2000). Executive coaching: An integrative model. *Dissertation Abstracts International, 61*, AAT 9971459.

Orenstein, R. L. (2002). Executive coaching: It's not just about the executive. *Journal of Applied Behavioral Science, 38*, 355–374.

Orenstein, R. L. (2006). Measuring executive coaching efficacy? The answer was right here all the time. *Consulting Psychology Journal: Practice and Research, 58*(2), 106–116.

Peterson, D. R. (1997). *Educating professional psychologists: History and guiding conception.* Washington, DC: American Psychological Association.

Rivera, P. R. (2002, September 29). Averting risks of coach craze. *The Boston Globe,* p. G2.

Saporito, T. J. (1996). Business-linked executive development: Coaching senior executives. *Consulting Psychology Journal, 48*(2), 96–103.

Shea, S. C. (1988). *Psychiatric interviewing: The art of understanding.* Philadelphia, PA: W. B. Saunders.

Singer, J. (1994). *Boundaries of the soul: The practice of Jung's psychology.* New York: Doubleday.

Sperry, L. (1993). Working with executives: Consulting, counseling, and coaching. *Individual Psychology, 49*(2), 257–266.

Sullivan, H. S. (1970). *The psychiatric interview.* New York: Norton.

Tobias, L. L. (1996). Coaching executives. *Consulting Psychology Journal, 48*(2), 87–95.

Van Steenberg LaFarge, V. (1995). Termination in groups. In J. Gillette & M. McCollom (Eds.), *Groups in context* (pp. 49–85). Lanham, MD: University Press.

Westen, D. (1990). Psychoanalytic approaches to personality. In L. Pervin (Ed.), *Handbook of personality theory and research* (pp. 21–63). New York: Guilford.

Whitmont, E. (1964). Group therapy and analytical psychology. *Journal of Analytical Psychology, 9*(1), 1–22.

Whyte, W. F., & Hamilton, E. L. (1965). *Action research for management: A case report on research and action in industry.* Homewood, IL: Richard D. Irwin.

Whyte, W. F., & Whyte, K. K. (1984). *Learning from the field: A guide from experience.* Beverly Hills, CA: Sage.

Winnicott, D. W. (1960). The theory of the parent-infant relationship. *International Journal of Psycho-analysis, 41,* 585-595.

Witherspoon, R., & White, R. P. (1996). Executive coaching: A continuum of roles. *Consulting Psychology Journal, 48*(2), 124–133.

Index

Clients (*Continued*)
  preliminary meetings, 47–48
  relationship with manager, 57–58,
    93, 160
  self-awareness in, 17, 100
Coaching. *See also* Executive coaching;
    Formal coaching process
Coaching, conclusion of
  case analysis, 140
  case study, 139–140
  early, 138
  reasons for, 137–139, 162
Coaching contracts
  boundary permeability and,
    65–67
  case analyses, 66–67
  case studies, 66
  components of, 65
  data gathered from, 65
  ownership by client, 65
Coaching failure, 143–150
  client factors, 143–144
  consultant factors, 147–149
  organizational factors, 145–147
  predicting, 149–150
Coaching pyramid, 100
Cognitive formations, 30
Cognitive interventions, 105–106
Conceptual framework, 25–34
  individual and organization in, 25,
    26–27
  multilevel forces in, 25, 29–31
  unconscious forces in, 25, 27–29
  use of self in, 25, 31–33
Conclusion of coaching
  case analysis, 140
  case study, 139–140
  early, 138
  reasons for, 137–139, 162
Confidentiality
  ethical implications of, 153–154
  in feedback process, 84
  institutional, 154
  in interview process, 73

  in objectives setting, 94
Conflict of interest, 154
Contracts. *See* Coaching contracts
Countertransference
  in case analyses, 112, 164, 165, 166, 168
  defined, 28, 31
  in formal coaching process, 106, 153
  in therapeutic process, 28, 31

Data analysis
  in Empathic Organic
    Questionnaire, 122
  feedback preparation, 83–84
Data gathering
  from coaching contracts, 65
  at entry, 36, 41, 160
  at initial contact, 36, 41, 42, 160
  at joint goal setting, 57–58, 160
  ongoing process of, 36–37
  in preliminary meeting process,
    47, 160
  through assessment, 71–74, 162
  through observation, 36, 71
Defense mechanisms
  in case analyses, 54, 63, 80, 90,
    112–113, 166, 168
  during assessment, 72, 73
  in formal coaching process, 106
  respecting, 106
Development, coaching for, 17
Diedrich, R. C., 16
Direct questions, in psychodynamic
  interviews, 72
Doyle, M., 16–17
Drath, W. H., 16
Dual relationships, 153
Dyadic method, in formal coaching, 106

Education/training, for coaches, 14, 15,
  151, 152, 153
Embedded intergroup relations theory,
  30–31, 159
Empathic Organic Questionnaire
  administration, 122

Dictionary of Health Economics and Finance

David Edward Marcinko, MBA, CFP, CMP
Hope Hetico, RN, MHA, CPHQ, Editors

An Essential Tool for Every Health Care Industry Sector:

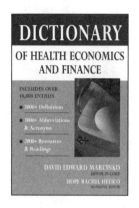

- Physician, provider, and health care facility
- Payer, intermediary, and insurance professional
- Layperson, purchaser, and benefits manager

Key Benefits & Features Include:

- New Terminology
- Abbreviations & Acronyms
- Illustrations
- Climetric Equations
- Cross-references to Research

"One needs to have the right words, and to use seemingly everyday terms in a way that economists and healthcare financial experts speak. Simply put, my suggestion is to refer to the Dictionary of Healthcare Economics and Finance frequently, and 'reap'."

—**Thomas E. Getzen,** PhD
Executive Director, International Health Economics Association (iHEA)
Professor of Risk, Insurance, and Healthcare Management
The Fox School of Business, Temple University

2006 · 264pp · Softcover · 978-0-8261-0254-6

11 West 42nd Street, New York, NY 10036-8002 • Fax: 212-941-7842
Order Toll-Free: 877-687-7476 • Order Online: www.springerpub.com